"I'm proud of Devin DeVasquez think her book *The Naked Truth abo* read and will be of interest to anyor photography." —**Hugh M. Hefner,**

"Devin is a most unique and unusual pinup. She is the only pinup model to have interviewed me. I think she's great 'cause she's a natural brunette, and I'm flattered that she's admired me and is doing a book on pinup modeling." —**Bettie Page, Pinup Legend**

"Devin DeVasquez is the essential pinup. She has oodles of beauty, brains, sexiness, and kindness. Her pinup book is a must-read for girls who aspire to be pinups and the boys who love them." —**Mamie Van Doren, Actress/Pinup Queen**

"Devin DeVasquez has natural beauty, charm, and elegance above all others. She has survived in Hollywood with her sharp wit and exotic, intoxicating looks. Her contributions to film, pinup glamour, and the art world are immeasurable. Devin is a dear friend and admired colleague. What I admire most about Devin is her sweetness and authenticity and, man, can she cook some serious southern gumbo!" —**Julie Strain, Queen of All Media**

"Well, what can I say about Devin? She is one of my favorite models/Playmates. She is truly timeless, always beautiful. How Devin keeps that body, I have no idea, but I'm glad she does! As far as pinup goes, the true pinup was before my time, although it too is timeless. I think there is a swing back to the pinup look. I guess the Playmate is a sort of modern pinup, although the centerfold is much sexier. I am glad to see the pinup making a comeback. I think it is a sexy and flattering way to look at women." —**Arny Freytag, Playboy Photographer**

"I have known Devin since I became a Playmate in 1996. She is one of the few Playmates and pinup models who embodies the two titles to a tee, then and now. Devin has some magic potion that keeps her from aging, I'm sure of it. I must get some! She is a pinup icon and from an artist's point of view one of the most gorgeous faces to render.

Not just a pretty face, Devin is smart, witty, and a hell of a cook. If pinup is an art form, then Devin is a Da Vinci." —**Victoria Fuller, Playboy Playmate/Pinup Artist**

"Devin DeVasquez, when I first met her, was this sweet, innocent, adorable, dark-haired beauty found by one David Chan at Playboy. You could not look at her and not be struck by her beauty. But the most remarkable thing of all is that Devin not only is still beautiful, but has now used that beauty to bring back the subtle art of pinup to women.

"With her still-amazing body, Devin personifies the pinup model physique. Her full, natural breasts are utterly gorgeous, and she still has great legs and all the rest to boot! I love working with her as she's completely comfortable in front of the camera and her personality always shows through in her images. With this combination and her zeal for the pinup of old, she becomes what we almost lost all those years ago during the age of Golden Hollywood, where the pinups reigned true everywhere and were seen painted on everything from walls to military planes at war. I wouldn't be surprised to see a painting of Devin on the fuselage of one of our modern fighter jets somewhere in the world today! She is a doll and will always remain one to me."
—**David Mecey, Former staff photographer of Playboy**

"For years I have admired Devin, before even knowing her and finding out what a wonderful friend she is too! I remember sitting home in New York and watching her win *Star Search*. It was then I told my dad, 'That's what I want to do!' Devin is an inspiration and has always impressed me with her ability to excel in everything she does with beauty and grace!. A true lady who doesn't compromise herself. I am proud to call Devin my friend today and walk through her home and feel the love and success she so deserves!" —**Sandra Taylor, Actress/Pinup Star**

"Devin DeVasquez was my first model, and I have been very inspired by her natural beauty and elegance." —**Michael Mobius, Pinup Artist**

"Devin is a real diva and pinup star, as well as a shrewd businesswoman that I'm inspired by. She's been a terrific friend of mine for many years, and I'm thrilled to be a part of the pinup world and Playboy. It's girls like us who keep glamour alive today and define what it will be in the future." —**Cindy Margolis, Internet Pioneer/Author/Pinup Star**

"I first met and photographed Devin in the '80s for *Playboy*. I remember at that time she was one of the most popular Playmates. She was also an incredible pinup model, making my job easy with her natural poses and expressions. I felt most fortunate to work with her. We became and remained friends over the years, getting together for occasional photo shoots or social engagements. I'm not surprised Devin has written a book on the mysterious world of pinup modeling. Very few models are as experienced as she is or as revealing. Devin has been there, seen it all, and can tell the story as no other." —**Ken Marcus, World-Renowned Glamour Photographer**

"Devin personifies what it is like to be a pinup legend. Bettie Page and I loved being around Devin to trade stories about the evolution of the pinup queens. I know Bettie was always so proud to call Devin her friend. I personally always thought Devin had the class, beauty, and dignity to help make the pinup queens the idols that they are today." —**Mark Roesler, Business Agent for Bettie Page and the Marilyn Monroe estate**

"Candid, open, and honest, Devin DeVasquez reveals the real truth about being a pinup model. Masterful at creating her own brand, Devin shares insights on how to use the Internet to its full capacity with tips, strategies, and techniques that everyone wanting to be a pinup model needs to know. Using her own personal experiences as references (and those of others, as relevant examples), you'll discover why this is one of the most enjoyable and informative books you'll ever read." —**Adam Ginsberg, America's Go-to Guy for Making Big Money on the Internet**

"I don't find choosing a model a clear-cut, easy thing. There are so many beautiful women and so many types of beauty. I chose Bettie over 30 years ago. I was just starting my career, and my friend had a stack of photos of her. I didn't know who she was, what she did, but she sure stood out among the other models—her energy, her smile, her look of pure enjoyment in front of the camera. Whatever Bettie was thinking, she truly was at a party in her own head. It would be easy to say it's Julie Strain's six-foot-two frame that makes her stand out, but I have seen her standing among other women, and they are moths driven to the flame. Larger than life, a big beautiful smile one moment and a vicious snarl the next, she is the grand Dame. Sandy Taylor, absolutely gorgeous and curvaceous, a real sex-pot. There are so many beautiful women, but this does not always translate to the camera. There is magic, and as any magician knows, it takes work to make it seem easy. Devin is a classic beauty, movie star looks, like a leading lady from the glamorous 1940s. Devin's beauty alone assures her status as a top Playboy model, but her creativity in front of the camera guarantees her enduring fame."
—Olivia, Pinup Artist

"When I think of Devin, I think of a woman with timeless beauty and talent. I had the privilege of being involved in a photo shoot years after her Playboy Playmate shoot and thought, 'this woman looks as beautiful today as she did for Playboy.' As an added benefit, she insisted on cooking for us after the shoot. Brains, beauty, and great cooking … perfect! The perfect pinup has the face of angelic innocence combined with the body of devilish experience." **—Bob Shultz, Glamourcon**

The Naked Truth About A Pinup Model

Devin DeVasquez

PersonaPublishing
1663 Liberty Drive
Bloomington, IN 47403
www.personapublishing.com
Phone: 1-800-839-8640

© *2009 Devin DeVasquez. All rights reserved.*

No part of this book may be reproduced, stored in a retrieval system, or transmitted by any means without the written permission of the author.

First published by PersonaPublishing   6/29/2009

ISBN: 978-1-6048-1528-3 (sc)

Printed in the United States of America
Bloomington, Indiana

This book is printed on acid-free paper.

The Naked Truth About A Pinup Model

Cover photograph of Devin DeVasquez by Ronn Moss.

For more information on this book or direct sales, please visit www.devindevasquez.com.

Dedication

This book is dedicated to Bettie Page for paving the way.

Acknowledgements

A special thank you to Mark Roesler for his inspiration in writing this book. Thank you to Ronn Moss, my husband and photographer. I would like to thank my Playboy family and Hugh Hefner, as well as the following friends and pinup legends of the future: Cindy Margolis, Dita Von Teese, Julie Strain, Mamie Van Doren, Delores Del Monte, Sandra Taylor, and Victoria Fuller. A special thanks to the following artists whom I have had the pleasure of inspiring and being inspired by: Olivia, Michael Mobius, Walter Girotto, and Jon Hul. Thank you to the following photographers and friends for their love and support, Arny Freytag, David Mecey, Ken Marcus, Bob Shultz and Adam Ginsberg . A final thanks to photographer David Chan, who discovered the pinup girl in me.

Contents

Dedication	ix
Acknowledgements	xi
Introduction	1
Chapter One: What Is A Pinup?	9
Chapter Two: Fantasy vs. Reality	29
Chapter Three: Maximizing Fame	41
Chapter Four: Uniquely You	55
Chapter Five: The Internet and Publicity	75
Chapter Six: Personal Appearances	97
Chapter Seven: Steps To Stardom	121
Chapter Eight: Branding An Icon	137
Chapter Nine: The Future of Pinup	147
Chapter Eleven: Anna Nicole Smith	151
Chapter Ten: A Conversation With Bettie	157
Author's Bio	177

Introduction

Over the past fifty years, pinup modeling has moved into the mainstream and is more popular today than ever before. The Internet has introduced a whole host of beautiful models to the world of pinup, and there are new ones surfacing every day.

Being sexy is considered money in the bank. Today's models are curvy, sexy women and are known for more than just their looks; some have even influenced high fashion. Stars like Jennifer Lopez and Anna Nicole Smith helped to make this change. Dita Von Teese brought back burlesque dancing with a passion and gave it a very elegant style. Pamela Anderson redefined what being blonde was all about, and super-sexy Victoria Silvstedt became a supermodel model.

Playboy magazine's Playmates seem to be everywhere these days, and young girls all over the world dream of becoming fantasy girls or pinups. Dreams of glamour and stardom make up what most pinup girls want to achieve.

The success of the hit TV show *The Girls Next Door* on the E channel has given eighty-four-year-old Hugh Hefner and his three pinup girlfriends instant television stardom. These girls can now go on and brand their image and names on a variety of product endorsements and connect to the world through the Internet.

And it all began with the pinup. Models such as Bettie Page, Marilyn Monroe, and Dita Von Teese all got their start in show business from pinup modeling. Success such as this shows what can be achieved in the pinup world today.

While growing up, never in my dreams did I think I wanted to become a pinup girl. But little did I know when I used to daydream about Hollywood stars that many of them would be attending my fortieth birthday party—a party equipped with paparazzi taking my pictures with men and women who idolized me just for taking my clothes off.

So how did I become one of the most elite women of fantasy, a model in the company of Marilyn Monroe, Bettie Page, Pamela Anderson, and Anna Nicole Smith? How did a poor ethnic southern girl come to date one of the most famous rock stars and movie stars of the twentieth century? How did my image come to be painted by pinup artists around the world and photographed by top photographers? How did I get invited to A-list parties and come to be fantasized about by millions?

It seems kind of surreal, my life. For more than half of it, I have been a pinup girl. Playboy discovered me while I was attending college at LSU. I was only seventeen at the time because I had graduated early from high school, and I was painfully shy and introverted. I was the girl least likely to become a fantasy girl for *Playboy*. Barely noticed in high school, I never participated in school activities, wasn't homecoming queen or a cheerleader, and hardly dated.

I thought *Playboy* was a classy magazine and remember my college English teacher bringing one in to discuss some of the articles. *Playboy* was in its own league as were its women and of course its creator, Hugh Hefner. I began to believe that I could create my own unique brand.

Coming from the south, I noticed that people could be quite hypocritical and narrow-minded in their views on nudity. I developed my own opinion—as I did with anything I attempted—and I decided that I wanted to become someone that my parents, grandparents, and future children would be proud of.

I remember feeling appalled by the fact that people judged me for posing nude. I was even fired from a job I had with the state's Department of Revenue, just because I decided to pose nude in college. They sure were sneaking the magazine in the bathroom to look at though. I had outgrown Baton Rouge and had enough courage to test for Playmate. The test for Playboy and facing rejection was scary in and of itself.

The process of becoming a Playmate is a lengthy one, and the possibility of rejection came early for me, but I was determined to make it because I had to. I was now tainted in the southerners' eyes, and so this seemed like a pretty good option—not to mention the $15,000 paycheck didn't hurt.

I was tired of working two part-time jobs and taking a full college schedule, and I was totally alone. Playboy gave me an instant family of interesting people and opened doors I could only have dreamed about.

Everything of course is about timing, and I guess I came along at the right time, for my look was unique and interesting enough for photographers to test me. *Flashdance* and *Purple Rain* were big hits at the box office, and I looked like the lead girls in those films. I was compared to Jennifer Beals, Vanity, and Apollonia so often it became irritating. I used to say, "One day, I just want someone to remember Devin DeVasquez."

As time went on, I became more confident and comfortable with posing nude and with Devin. Things had really changed in the twenty-first century, and I decided to give myself to the world through my Web site. Pinups were more in the mainstream thanks to Pamela Anderson and Anna Nicole Smith, among others. Devin now had babies named after her and was fast becoming a legend in the pinup world.

Just making the decision to pose nude changed my life forever and made me an instant celebrity. *Playboy* opened doors for me to model, act, and sign autographs for fans. It was a little overwhelming to adapt to this new life. I just wanted to be in love with a man who wanted to have a family, the family I never had growing up.

I never knew my real father, had a mentally ill mother, and lived in foster homes and through sexual abuse. I changed my name and got a nose job. I guess I wanted to become someone else. These were similarities between me and other pinup legends like Marilyn, Bettie, and Jean Harlow.

Another thing most pinup legends seem to have in common is that there can never be enough love for them. I felt the same; I desperately wanted someone to love me the way I dreamed of being loved. I feared

I'd die young or simply never experience it; love was so important to me.

Unfortunately, loving relationships are hard to come by for pinup models. Men can become insanely jealous or abusive of a girlfriend who is a pinup, yet incredibly attracted to the fact that they have such a trophy. That makes it hard to have stable, nurturing relationships, as history has shown with Marilyn, Bettie, and Jean.

I think that Hef is the only living person who has documented and videotaped his entire dream to share with the world. Playboy is a worldwide logo, and Hef is recognized as the grandfather of the sexual revolution. Everyone now wants to be a part of the rabbit and what it stands for, which is the freedom to be who you are and who you want to be, and that's about as American as it gets.

But what exactly is a pinup, and how do you become a successful pinup model? What makes a pinup a legend? How do you capitalize on the fame that usually lasts such a short time for most pinups? How do you brand that name that is known to millions? What is reality, and what is fantasy? That's what this book is all about—the definitive handbook on how to become a successful pinup.

I have spent half of my life as a pinup model and watched the changes in the industry along the way. I know very well this world of which I speak. It is a very unique and interesting world indeed. Whether you want to be a pinup model or are just curious about what being a pinup model is all about, here you will find the "Naked Truth about A Pinup Model."

This book is a look at my twenty-five-year experience as a successful pinup model, and how I maximized my celebrity status by branding my name and image. It will give you insight into this exclusive world and help you carve your own niche in history, if you so desire.

I wrote this book as a guide to help future pinups achieve success and prolong their celebrity status into the future. I'll show you how to make a career from it for years to come. I'll help you learn how to break into film and television the right way, and how to keep your fans loyal to you. You will understand how to achieve success as a pinup that could make you a legend in the future.

I believe in creative visualization and that we all have the capabilities to create our own realities. Hugh Hefner did it; Marilyn Monroe did it; and so did I. You must first believe in yourself and then others will believe in you. I want to share my knowledge and experience with you in hopes that you will be inspired to know you can live out your dreams!

Recent modeling photo

DEVIN DE VASQUEZ
MISS JUNE 1985

DEVIN DE VASQUEZ
MISS JUNE 1985

Chapter One: What Is A Pinup?

The New Merriam-Webster Dictionary defines a pinup as: "suitable for pinning up on an admirer's wall (photo); also, suited (as by beauty) to be the subject of a pinup photograph." But what exactly is a pinup? Who is she, and what does it mean to be a pinup?

The idea of a pinup girl started during World War II with women such as Betty Grable. Soldiers fighting wanted to remember what they had waiting for them at home in America and would put photos of girls from magazines up in their lockers and on their walls as that reminder. They were usually cheesecake poses that evoked fantasy in most men.

In 1953, Hugh Hefner started a new and controversial men's magazine called *Playboy*, and its first cover girl and centerfold was none other than the sexiest woman of that time, Marilyn Monroe. She epitomized the pinup girl in all her natural glory and gave the men a new way to view their fantasy.

Marilyn was of course nude, and *Playboy* became an instant success, making Hugh Hefner's lifestyle the envy of most men. *Playboy* also set the standard for what a pinup girl was, is, and always will be: "the ultimate fantasy" or "the girl next door," as Hugh Hefner coined.

The pinup girl embodied the fantasy of the girl next door that most men dreamed about and hoped to meet someday. She seemed flawless and untouchable to many, which made her all the more desired.

Soon after Marilyn, another pinup girl grabbed the spotlight. She was a beautiful brunette with bright blue eyes and a style all her own. She captured the pinup world and was to become their "Pinup Queen." America became infatuated with Bettie Page.

Bettie always seemed to be having fun in her photos. Her bright smile drew you in, and her popularity grew fast. Bettie was also the first to pose in bondage and fetish photos, which were rare and controversial in the 1950s.

Her career became extremely controversial when she was asked to testify against her employer, Irving Klaw, before the US Senate Committee in an investigation against Klaw. She disappeared shortly afterwards, and for decades, stories emerged as to what had happened to this pinup queen. Her exile made her a legend, and she inspired supermodels, photographers, artists, designers, and rock stars to copy her style and image. Bettie's images and her mysterious disappearance kept the pinup girl alive, and the future generation fans of pinup made her their queen.

Over three decades later, Bettie was found as an old lady living in Florida, unaware that she was a living legend. I had the privilege to interview her a few years ago for a pinup documentary I was working on and found her to be just as interesting as she was in her early years. She told me that she was called a "slut and a harlot" and everything in between for posing nude in the 1950s, because there were just not many girls doing it at that time. I was the first pinup to ever interview her, and that has been the highlight of my pinup career. (Excerpts from the interview can be found later in this book.)

The "pinup girl" is in a league of her own. As you can see, there is a distinct difference between Marilyn's image and Bettie's, but they both bring to mind beauty and sexiness. Other pinups followed Marilyn and Bettie, but none with the essence that they possessed, for they were the pioneers of it all.

The sexual revolution took place as the 1960s rolled around. *Playboy* continued to flourish and brand their bunny in the famous nightclubs. It seemed everyone wanted to be a part of the lifestyle, and Hugh Hefner threw the most lavish and erotic parties, with pinups galore.

Suddenly, all of Hollywood followed and the "pinup girl" became something that wasn't real to most people. *Playboy* countered this with a data sheet that listed her "turn-ons" and "turn-offs," her measurements, and her birthplace, but she still seemed artificial.

How do you meet a girl like her, many wondered? What is she really like? *Playboy* claimed she was "the girl next door," but was she? Did girls really look like that?

Photography had a lot to do with the classic *Playboy* style and image of the Playboy Playmate. The girls were portrayed as sweet and innocent girls next door who liked sex—the girls that most men dreamed of meeting.

As each decade rolled by, the pinup girl changed and got bolder and more confident in the way she was portrayed. Photography changed along with body types, and America's views changed too. Eventually, pinup girls were seen in mainstream movies, television programs, and magazines. It seemed that each decade introduced at least one pinup that the public wanted to see more of.

Mainstream actresses began posing for *Playboy* as did fashion models and "supermodels" to boost their careers. The idea of what it meant to be a pinup began to change.

As *Playboy* turned fifty years old, Bettie and Marilyn became well-known legends. Looking back, it is apparent who stood out from the elite group of women who graced the magazine, but who are the legends of tomorrow? What makes them stand apart from the rest, and where will the pinup be in the future?

I believe that with the Internet there will be more pinups to admire in the future, and if a girl is smart, the opportunities from posing nude today can create residual income for the future. A great example of this is model Dita Von Teese, born as Heather Sweet. Dita had a love for the 1940s and '50s, and although she was a natural blonde, she dyed her hair jet black so that the contrast against her snow-white skin would give her that old movie star allure. She styled herself to represent the era by dressing in vintage clothing and even drove a vintage car. She really lived it, so it wasn't an act to her. Dita started her own Web site devoted to her love of photos from that era, which she emulated.

She performed her now-famous burlesque shows around the globe and made a name for herself. Hugh Hefner came to see her show one night and offered her a *Playboy* cover and pictorial. Dita now has a cult following and is often compared to Bettie Page. She was married to rock star Marilyn Manson, and models today now emulate her style of corsets and glamour. Dita will be a legend in the future. Her love for glamour and that era served as a path for Dita to become who she is today.

Maybe you want to cultivate your own unique aura in photos? This is what a pinup does; she sets the standard for others to copy and follow. Perhaps you have a love for the 60s and want to be the next Jayne Mansfield? It's okay to take cues from the previous pinups of yesterday and make it your own today. That's what Dita did; she admired and emulated Bettie Page and the pinups from that era and made up her own style in the process for future generations to follow. What Dita did shows that you don't have to be a Playboy Playmate to make a name for yourself—but having the Playboy stamp of approval doesn't hurt either.

Like the past fifty years, the next fifty years will have its own set of legends, such as Pamela Anderson, Anna Nicole Smith, and others we haven't met yet, for generations to admire. The pinup girl is here to stay, and her power will just grow stronger over time. The pinup girl conveys beauty, glamour, and the freedom to be a seductive woman who knows the power of all that she is. The pinup girl has evolved into a twenty-first-century woman who is in control of her destiny, and what she wants out of life is hers for the taking.

My own experience as a pinup girl has been a great one. I was a poor child from the deep south of Baton Rouge, Louisiana, and grew up in various foster homes. I never dreamed I'd be a pinup model. But somehow I was discovered by *Playboy*. I found that I photographed well, and to be chosen by *Playboy* gave me tremendous self-confidence. I went on to become Miss June 1985 and graced the cover in November of 1986 after I won $100,000 on the hit TV show *Star Search* as their champion spokesmodel.

My modeling and acting career took off, as I did countless national commercials for companies such as Coca-Cola, Burger King, and Miller Brewing Company. This led to movies such as *Can't Buy Me Love*, *House 2*, *Society*, and *Low Down Dirty Shame*.

I gained knowledge that college couldn't teach me, as I traveled the globe to do autograph shows, talk shows, and promotional appearances for *Playboy*. I have been a part of a worldwide brand that everyone knows and respects. Playboy has become a family to me, and the girls have become sorority sisters whom I have grown up with.

I know that I will be remembered in the future for the images I have given to the many fans, and I feel honored and grateful to have been given this blessing in my life. I'm proud to be a pinup girl.

Every girl has a different reason for wanting to do pinup modeling. Maybe it's a love of glamour. Maybe she found her father's *Playboys* when she was a teenager and wanted to be a Playmate. Maybe she wants to be a starlet and then a star on the silver screen or marry a rock star. Whatever the reason, I can tell you being a pinup model is a very unique and powerful experience. Once you are a pinup model, your life is never the same. Posing nude brings out a certain sexual power, and the freedom to be naked for millions of people to see is provocative in and of itself.

The love of pinup is hotter than ever. Pinup models are supermodels today, with an ever-growing fan base of mostly men. However, more and more women are getting into pinup; even collecting pinup photos and pinup art has become more popular.

This shows an understanding of how truly powerful women are in the twenty-first century. Bettie and Marilyn's era gave little power to what they represented. It has only been throughout the past few decades that they have become the icons they are today.

Few women posed nude back then, and those who did were looked down on for doing it. Religion and society did not accept what they called pornography. Bettie Page, being the first to pose in fetish and bondage photos, thus caused a controversy. A young boy hung himself, and his brother blamed this on the fact that his brother loved and tried to re-create Bettie's bondage photos.

This was depicted in *The Notorious Bettie Page*, an HBO movie about Bettie's life. I saw a private screening of it with Bettie and a small group of friends at the Playboy Mansion. Bettie became very emotional during the screening and obviously didn't feel this accusation about her photos was truthful.

I put myself in her shoes and imagined watching my life story at eighty-two years old—my own pinup career and trials and triumphs there for everyone to view and talk about. The pain and backlash she got from posing nude at that time must have been hard to endure, even though she enjoyed being a pinup model.

Bettie told me she always had fun doing her shoots and that she'd made her own costumes, such as the bullet bra, which Madonna has been known to wear on stage. Bettie felt good about her body because she worked out with weights and swam regularly, and she loved to dance. She loved showing off her beautiful physique and getting paid for it!

Camera clubs were very popular during Bettie's era and gave fans a chance to take nude photos of their favorite pinup girls. Bettie was the most popular, of course, and the camera clubs loved her. A small group of camera bugs would gather around a model like Bettie and shoot various poses of her for their private portfolios.

Throughout the past few decades, the views on posing nude, especially for *Playboy*, have clearly changed drastically from Bettie's era. Body types have also changed. Most pinup models now have had breast augmentations, whereas in the '50s and '60s, the natural breasts were more popular. Today natural breasts are a rarity, and since I have natural breasts, I decided to market my brand to that effect.

The pinup girl today is still evolving. Because the Internet is breeding them faster than ever, no longer is *Playboy* introducing them exclusively. Many beautiful magazines are on the market today such as *FHM, Stuff,* and *Maxim*, featuring gorgeous models in sexy lingerie, swimsuits, or next to nothing as the industry's "it girl."

These new men's magazines feature pinups, and a lot of these women also pose nude in *Playboy*. Several are featured in movies and television, or have Web sites. So there is more of a crossover for the pinup girls of the present. The pinup is no longer limited to Playboy photos, but has more choices in other venues of the entertainment industry. This of course helps to brand her name and image on a variety of products.

How To Find The Pinup In You:

1. Experiment with various hair and makeup styles. Remember, pinup is glamour.

2. Practice a variety of famous pinup poses. You can get old pinup books to use as references, and even make up some new ones of your own. Practice daily in front of a mirror.

3. Decide on a catchy and unique name for yourself. Most pinups have changed their names.

4. Go to a vintage clothing store and develop a style of dressing; you can mix and match things from the past and the present for your own unique look. Remember, the sky is the limit and you must create your own interesting look and vibe.

5. Get some photographs taken to see if you are photogenic and what your strengths and weaknesses are, as well as to practice posing.

6. Consult a plastic surgeon if necessary to fine-tune what is needed.

7. Consult a personal trainer or join a gym and stay fit and toned.

8. Practice good feminine manners when in public; a pinup is always a lady.

9. Maintain a good, balanced diet.

10. Believe in yourself, and others will too.

My "All American" pinup pose

Dita Von Teese

Dita Von Teese, Debra Jo Fondren, and Devin

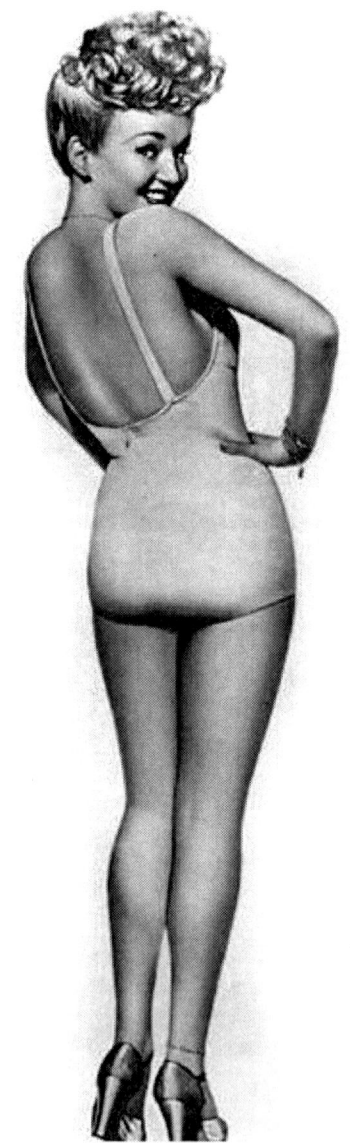

Betty Grable

Betty Grable

Marilyn Monroe

Marilyn Monroe

Marilyn Monroe

Bettie Page

Bettie Page

Mamie Van Doren

Mamie Van Doren

Chapter Two: Fantasy vs. Reality

We know that the pinup girl is, for the most part, fantasy. Her photos are posed, and the photography is often glamorous and seductive in dream settings. Few people know girls like this, and that makes their centerfolds tacked on the walls even more of a fantasy. The reality, of course, is that they are real girls, and having been one myself, I can attest to the fact that I am made of flesh and blood, not celluloid.

I have been asked many times about the realities of Hugh Hefner, the mansion, and other centerfolds. It seems people are still curious as to what the lifestyle and the girls are really like.

Do the girls really write what is on their data sheets? That was a frequently asked question I used to get when I first became a Playmate. The answer is yes. I know I did; it was another way to bring me into reality.

Another misconception is that all the photos are airbrushed, and the girls don't really look like they do in the photos. That is not true, although only the centerfold itself is airbrushed, as to give it that flawless, perfect look. The girl has to be photogenic; some people photograph differently than they look in person. She must have breasts that look good in photos no matter how big or small.

Whether she is short or tall, curvy or narrow is not as important. These things can be taken care of with wardrobe and settings. However, finding a great face and breasts is like finding a needle in a haystack.

I once scouted for *Playboy* and went to strip clubs searching for fresh faces that could be models and never found one. College campuses were another place that *Playboy* scouted, and that's where photographer David Chan found me.

What are these girls like? Are they sex-crazed, and do they all sleep with Hugh Hefner? The fantasy of the Playboy Mansion has kept that question buzzing for as long as I can remember. I have friends who tell me they are asked all the time what I'm really like. The truth is, I'm a homebody geek who moonlights as a pinup star. I love to cook and entertain, read, and hike, and I even get a pimple once in a while.

I have never slept with Hugh Hefner, although I was once propositioned to join him and his then girlfriend Carrie Leigh for a swing session after a movie one night. I declined and was afraid to hang out at the mansion too much. Don't get me wrong; everyone there is on their best behavior, and it's a great place to hang out—not to mention the twenty-four-hour butler service—but I was very shy and just didn't partake in swinging. Some girls though didn't have my reservations and hung out frequently, sunbathing nude and mingling with stars like James Caan, Tony Curtis, and a host of other screen stars.

The reality is that Mr. Hefner is an upstanding, polite, and gracious man whom everyone loves to be around. He makes you feel welcome in his home and is really loyal to his friends. But he happens to be a swinger and loves multiple women. He's honest about it, and like the sign says on his bedroom door, "If you don't swing, don't ring."

I personally will always be grateful that he picked me to become Miss June 1985 and that he's become a dear friend. I once had the privilege of entertaining him at a dinner party; I couldn't believe I was entertaining the world's greatest entertainer.

He truly throws the best parties I have ever been to in my life. The Playboy Mansion parties are legendary. The decor is amazing, and the parties are filled with celebrities and beautiful women scantily clad—painted ladies, as they are called, who are nude, covered only by body paint, that walk around offering you yummy foods that tease your taste buds. Hugh Hefner made his wildest fantasies come true in the Playboy Mansion. The line between fantasy and reality is an extremely fine one for him.

A pinup, in reality, is a real woman who evokes fantasy. It is sometimes hard to separate what is real from what is fantasy in this world. I have had men try to date me just because I'm a Playboy Playmate. Some men want so badly to go to the Playboy Mansion and think that dating a Playmate is a ticket to the realization of their dreams and fantasies.

When I was a Playmate, we were not allowed to have husbands or boyfriends attend the Playboy parties. Playboy wanted the Playmates to be available and approachable for the stars and friends of Hugh Hefner. Some Playmates would try to sneak their boyfriends into the mansion in the trunks of their cars! This of course didn't work, and those who tried to bend the rules were banned from future parties there.

Today, there is strict security at the Playboy Mansion. You must show your photo identification and get stamped and tagged by a Playboy official before you're shuttled up to the grounds. They do not invite every Playmate to every party, and those who are invited must request Mr. Hefner's approval of a guest. The request usually includes a photo of the guest.

Once a girl posed as me and called the mansion asking to bring her friends to a party. She talked to the butlers and even got through to Hef! Since I had never had a phone conversation with Mr. Hefner, I was surprised when he informed me of this imposter. Apparently, they all knew she was not me, but was curious as to who she was. She got angry and threatening when she couldn't get an approval from them. At the next party, I had to show identification and personally show myself to someone who knew me before entering. I was amused that someone would try to impersonate me.

These days, the mansion gets a slew of pranks and people who will go to great lengths to get into a Playboy party. I have even been offered money by high-powered businessmen to take them as my date to a party. They do not realize how difficult it is to get a man into the mansion! It's a lot easier to get a man approved for a mansion party if he's a celebrity, and even then, there is still the process of approval.

Another fantasy is that there are naked women walking around and orgies are going on all over the place, especially in the grotto. This of course is not true, but there have been times in the Playboy Mansion's history that some of these things did take place. I personally never saw these things during my pinup reign. It is still common to have girls sunbathing nude and naked people in the grotto. The torrid days of sex and orgies were in the '60s and '70s, according to stories I've heard from older Playmates. Each decade represented a different view on sex, and my era of the mid '80s was the worst period in Playboy's history.

Hefner had a stroke just before I became a centerfold, and the bunny clubs were closing down. Playboy had lost its casinos, and AIDS made everyone nervous about casual sex. My issue was being taken off the shelves of the 7-Elevens because of the Meece commission and the views of those in the Bible belt. Playboy wasn't sure if it would even make it another year.

Hefner turned over control of the magazine to his daughter, Christy Hefner, and advertisers were dropping off, so the magazine started to lose money. On top of everything, Hefner decided to get married! Everyone thought the party was over.

Playmates were not sunbathing nude around the mansion anymore, as babies and toys took over the grounds. Hef's friends began to disappear, and the pajama parties were replaced with black-tie events.

Today it's nice to see that things have come full circle, and the magazine is still respected and admired by a new generation. The birth of reality television has given us an insight into Hef's personal life with his current three girlfriends. This is not conventional or traditional television, but it sure is entertaining!

For instance, Playmate Anna Nicole Smith shocked us with her reality series when she weighed almost 300 pounds, and we witnessed her outrageous behavior. Many wondered if this reality TV would stand the test of time, and it seems to be doing so. Other pinups followed with their own reality series such as Carmen Electra and Shaina Moakler. It seems pinups and Playmates are all over the television set these days, showing us all who they really are.

Pamela Anderson went from *Baywatch* fame to her own FOX series *VIP*, which she produced and starred in. She became a regular in the tabloids due to her on-again, off-again marriage to rock star Tommy Lee. Pam later showed us how reality really meets fantasy. Pam has her own cartoon character, a bestselling book that was comically based on her life, and her own sitcom, *Stacked*, in which she again stars and produces. Pamela and Tommy's sex life also became public knowledge when their infamous sex tape was stolen and posted for public view on the Internet. Pam and Tommy sued and got millions from this controversial court case, but it didn't hurt Pam's career. She has appeared on the cover of *Playboy* more times than any other centerfold, and the public can't get enough of her.

These well-known pinups show how much the public accepts and embraces the seductiveness of the pinup girl today. No longer is she secluded and limited in what she can achieve. The sky is the limit, and she can do whatever she chooses, baring it all and offering no apologies and accepting no judgments for doing so. She is in control of her destiny and is no longer ridiculed for the decision to take it all off.

The reality of wanting people to approve of you is common. Most pinups come from small towns or conservative backgrounds. I remember how hypocritical I thought the deep south of Louisiana to be when I made the decision to pose nude. I was working as a student worker at the state's Department of Revenue in Baton Rouge, Louisiana, and lost my job when I first appeared in *Playboy* in 1981. I was an excellent worker and was always on time. It came as a shock when I was fired for no apparent reason soon after my topless photo appeared in the "Girls of the SEC" college pictorial. Boy, have things changed since then! Still there are many close-minded individuals who stand in judgment of such freedom to bare it all.

I think this is what made me want to become a Playmate and gave me the confidence to move away from such small minds. The odds against me were great, as I was one of the first Latin Playmates to grace the cover with my *Star Search* pictorial. My own success as a pinup came from a drive to be the best I could be with my opportunities.

Every pinup has a different reason for wanting to bare it all; mine was freedom—the freedom to become a beautiful, sexy woman in control of her destiny. It still remains one of the best decisions of my life. I have met, dated, befriended, and worked with some of the most interesting people in the world; my pinup career opened many doors that wouldn't have been opened otherwise.

I became a fantasy girl, and the reality was that I was still just a sweet little southern girl in a dreamland learning what this unique title meant. I didn't realize at the time that I would be a part of American history because of my Playboy Playmate title and what Playboy has become today.

I watched supermodels such as Cindy Crawford, Elle Macpherson, and Stephanie Seymour pose in *Playboy* pictorials. It became "vogue" to pose nude. Fantasy girls appeared in music videos, and many dated rock stars. It almost went hand in hand for a Playmate or a supermodel to date a rock star.

The pairing of KISS rocker Gene Simmons and Playmate of the Year Shannon Tweed was the most gossiped about. Then there was of course Pam and Tommy, along with Carmen Electra and Dave Navarro. These were super-sexy couples that brought together the fantasy of pinup and the bad boys of rock 'n' roll for everyone to drool over.

I dated *Purple Rain* star and mysterious musician Prince during his *Purple Rain* tour, just before I became Miss June 1985. I was introduced to him by Playboy, while shooting my "small camera" pictures for my centerfold pictorial. Photographer Richard Fegley was a big fan and played the *Purple Rain* album during our shoot. I didn't know much about Prince myself. Richard kept saying I looked like Apollonia, who also starred with Prince in the movie *Purple Rain*. Prince happened to be performing in the area, and Richard thought it would be natural for Prince to want to have his picture taken with a Playmate for the upcoming pictorial.

Richard arranged for us to go to the Prince concert in hopes of getting this photo of Prince and me. We went to the security people, and Richard showed them his Playboy identification and explained that I was an upcoming Playmate. He went on to request that we get a photo with Prince. We were politely informed that Prince didn't like to take photos and then sent home.

The next day, Richard and I were shooting more photos. It really bothered him that we hadn't gotten the photo with Prince. He just didn't want to take no for an answer. He had Playboy's publicity department contact Prince's publicity people to try to arrange a meeting.

They quickly summoned me, and I went with a Playboy secretary in tow. We heard the same thing about Prince not wanting to take photos, but I was invited to see the Purple Rain concert. Just before leaving, a bodyguard saw and approached me, asking to see my portfolio of modeling photos I was carrying. I reluctantly gave up my precious portfolio that I had worked so diligently on to the bodyguard. He took the photos to Prince, and he asked to meet me.

I was then picked up in a limo and placed in the first row at his concert that evening. I had never been in the first row of a concert in my life! Since I had seen the show the night before with Richard, I knew what to expect. I thought he was the most erotic and interesting performer I'd ever seen, and I saw a little too much of him when he split his skintight pants on stage during a dance split. Since I was in the first row and he was playing directly to me, this was quite comical.

After the concert, I was asked to allow Prince to go back to his hotel to shower and change his clothing before our meeting and to ride to the hotel with members of the crew in a van. It was late and I was getting tired; it had taken pretty much all day to try to get this photo with Prince, so I agreed.

Snow covered this chilly Chicago night, and suddenly the van did a double loop in three lanes of traffic, crashing into a median. I remember thinking I was going to die and never see the thousands of photos I had taken for *Playboy*, all because I was trying to get a photo with this elusive Prince. I hit my head and smelled gasoline, as someone pulled me out of the van. The crew and I hitchhiked to the hotel, and I was taken to a room to relax. By this time, my knees were shaking from the thought that I could have been killed!

I really couldn't stand up, so I was lying down on the bed with my eyes closed, trying to calm down. Just as I felt calm, I was shaken. I opened my eyes to find Prince looking down at me. He seemed shy and hardly looked at me as he extended his tiny lace-gloved hand to say hello. I thought he was so different from the Prince I'd just seen on stage.

I sat up quickly and explained what had happened in the accident. He asked where I was from and got excited when I told him Louisiana, because his father was from Louisiana as well. I told him about our quest for a photo with him and was told the same thing everyone else had been saying all along: he didn't like to take photos. I couldn't believe all that I'd gone through that day for a photo that I never got!

Prince invited me to a birthday party for Sheila E, but I had to decline because I was off to Los Angeles the next day. I had to do some more *Playboy* shooting and was going to visit the mansion and Hef for the first time.

This Prince meeting was memorable, and I couldn't believe what a week I was having. To meet Prince and then Hugh Hefner the next day—boy, this didn't seem real, but it was now my reality.

Of course, I didn't know what being a pinup would mean but found out that it meant lots of parties and pretty much anything you could fantasize your reality to be. My own fantasy was coming true with Playboy, and the reality of my new world was making me grow up pretty fast. The rest, as they say, is history.

Understanding What Is Fantasy And Reality In Your World:

1. Create a fantasy image but maintain the reality of your life.

2. Dress up because you love to and not to please others.

3. See that the pinup image is entertainment and nothing more.

4. Experiment with your pinup image at parties and have fun with it.

5. Incorporate your pinup image into your lifestyle, but keep it real. Remember, there is a time and place for everything.

6. Don't be starstruck by celebrities; remember, they are people just like you.

Playboy centerfold headshot

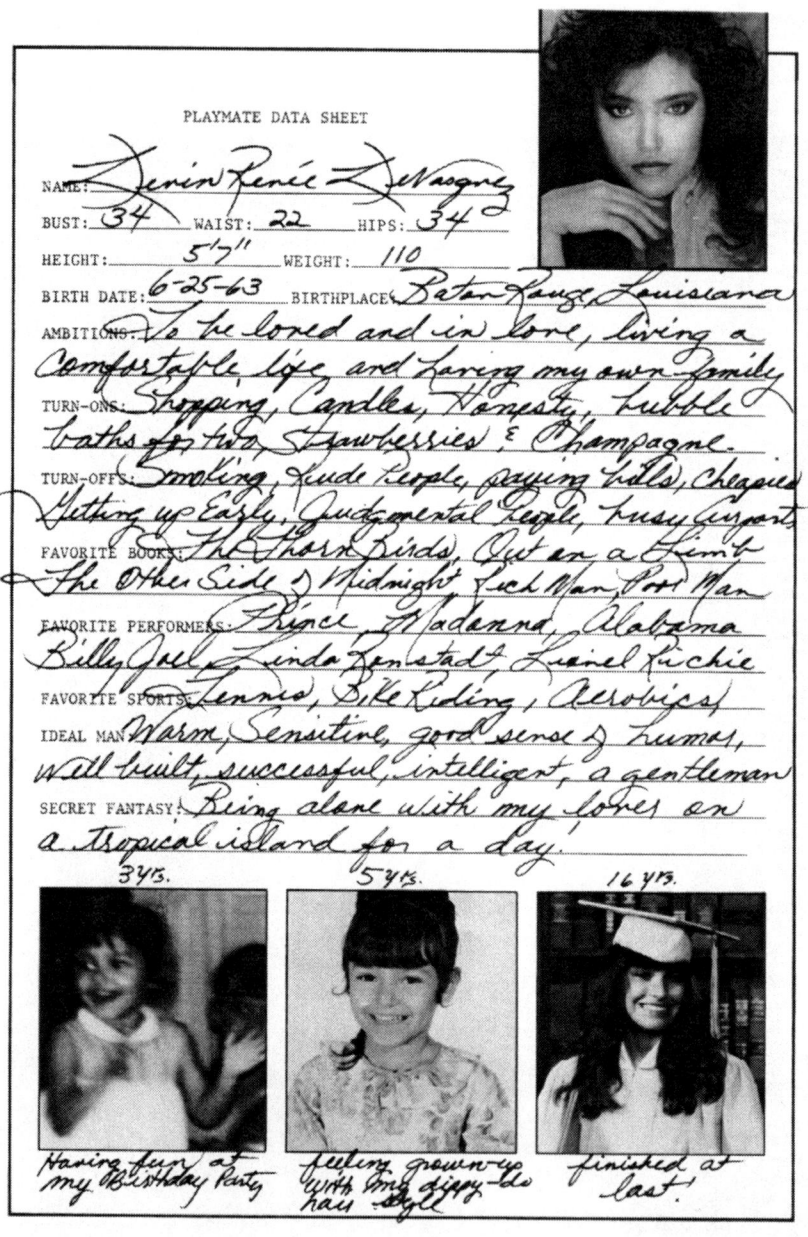

PLAYMATE DATA SHEET

NAME: Devin Renée DeVasquez
BUST: 34 WAIST: 22 HIPS: 34
HEIGHT: 5'7" WEIGHT: 110
BIRTH DATE: 6-25-63 BIRTHPLACE: Baton Rouge, Louisiana
AMBITIONS: To be loved and in love, living a comfortable life, and having my own family
TURN-ONS: Shopping, Candles, Honesty, bubble baths for two, Strawberries & Champagne.
TURN-OFFS: Smoking, Rude People, paying bills, cheapies, Getting up Early, Judgmental People, busy airports
FAVORITE BOOKS: The Thorn Birds, Out on a Limb, The Other Side of Midnight, Rich Man Poor Man
FAVORITE PERFORMERS: Prince, Madonna, Alabama, Billy Joel, Linda Ronstadt, Lionel Richie
FAVORITE SPORTS: Tennis, Bike Riding, Aerobics
IDEAL MAN: Warm, Sensitive, good sense of humor, well built, successful, intelligent, a gentleman
SECRET FANTASY: Being alone with my lover on a tropical island for a day.

3 yrs. — Having fun at my Birthday Party
5 yrs. — feeling grown up with my dippy-do hair style
16 yrs. — finished at last!

My Playboy data sheet

Chapter Three: Maximizing Fame

The reign of the average pinup is very short. If you are lucky enough to grace the pages of *Playboy* as a Playmate, it will give you instant fame. You are that month's fantasy girl, and everyone is buzzing about you. You become sought after for your pictures and autographs. Movie stars, rock stars, producers, and directors in Hollywood want to meet you. You get invited to lots of celebrity events, and doors that wouldn't normally open for you are flung wide open, for you are a starlet, living in a fantasy world. However, the reign in the limelight doesn't last long; there is another girl coming up next month.

So how does the pinup girl maximize that fame to last for years and even become a legend? Pinups are part of an elite group. There aren't many to begin with, and even fewer are remembered for years to come. The doors that quickly open for the average pinup can just as quickly close once her reign is over. It is important to prepare for the fame that comes with posing nude and make sure you know what you want to do with it beforehand.

Most pinups are young and naive to what exactly being a pinup means and entails. My hope in writing this book is to help future pinups understand this unique industry and find their own niche in this competitive market. The first step in maximizing your fame is to find out what makes you and your image unique.

In my case, I was a natural exotic pinup in a world of busty blondes. I carefully chose roles that went against the typical when doing films. For instance, I think I was the only Playboy Playmate to work for Walt Disney; I appeared in the high school comedy *Can't Buy Me Love* in 1987.

It is important to start carving the niche as early as possible. I always looked younger than my age, so playing high school roles when I was in my early twenties was the path I chose to go down. Other pinups continued to do sexy films. For instance, 1981 "Playmate of the Year" Shannon Tweed became the "Queen of the B Movies" when she starred in made-for-video movies with actor Andrew Stevens. Andrew's mother was a '60s Playmate, Stella Stevens, and she was one of the few actresses to break into the mainstream during her decade. If your desire is to become a mainstream actress, it is important to perhaps shy away from nudity and choose roles that go against the pinup image.

The next step in maximizing your fame is to keep your name in the public eye as much as possible. Some pinups change their names for their pinup career and use a different name for their acting or mainstream modeling career. I don't think that is really necessary today. Having the public familiar with your name and image helps to engrave it into their minds.

Whether you are the blonde bombshell, the elegant sophisticate, the retro exotic, or the feisty redhead, there is a market for your image today. It's a matter of knowing what your strengths and weaknesses are, and how you want the public to view you.

My fans know and love me as the natural, sexy, and alluring brunette. I recently went blonde just to experience what it was like, since most pinups seem to be blonde. I found that people not only treated me differently, but that my fans really couldn't wait for me to go back to brunette. It just didn't suit me as well. Can you imagine Pam Anderson going brunette? We know and love her so much as a blonde, right?

There is much more opportunity with the expansion of cable, the Internet, and the fact that pinups are all over mainstream television, movies, and magazines today. The possibilities are endless, so it's really up to the model to make intelligent choices early in her career.

The Naked Truth About A Pinup Model

The final step in maximizing the fame of being a pinup is to brand the name and image on products and merchandise. Once the image and name are recognized, this is very easy to do.

It is important to take charge of your brand and associate it with products and merchandise that can continue selling your image for years to come. Today, the World Wide Web enables us to communicate with millions of people, and it seems everyone has a Web site. This is an excellent and mandatory tool to have if you wish to be a pinup. You can personally choose what images you wish to give to fans all over the world, allowing you to cultivate and carve your own niche in the world of pinup. The type of products and merchandise depends on you and how you want to promote yourself.

In my case, at forty-five I'm more marketable now than I was when I was a Playmate at twenty-one. Ethnic models are more mainstream, and there is a whole slew of Latin stars on the scene today, such as Jennifer Lopez and Selma Hayek. This has paved the way for my name to endorse more mainstream products, as well as create my own. I have companies that deal with nutrition, beauty, lingerie, wine, and art associated with my brand. My name has been connected with pinup for over twenty-five years now. The image I have carved is one of exotic, erotic, and sophisticated allure.

Many young girls seek me out for advice about embarking in the world of Playboy, and the bigger their brands get, the bigger mine gets. I believe that pinup is here to stay, and pinups will have even more opportunities in the future to brand themselves. I see the surge of beauties willing to bare it all, without the bat of an eye, popping up every day.

The women of *Playboy* are widely recognized and sought after for liquor, lingerie, and beauty ads. Artists, photographers, and graphic designers seek out pinup models as their muses. The beauties who stand the test of time and have something special will prevail. If you are lucky enough to be one of the pinups that stand out, you can maximize that fame for the rest of your life. The fan base that a pinup has follows her forever.

I experienced a very sweet and touching situation recently that told me just what it means to be a pinup. I was signing autographs at

Glamourcon, a convention dedicated to pinup glamour, with several well-known pinups from the past and present in attendance.

Many loyal fans come to visit this show, especially to chat with and buy merchandise from their favorite pinup. One such fan was a navy lieutenant top gun commander, who was dressed in his white uniform and carrying a folded US flag under his arm. He was wandering around the convention, obviously looking for someone in particular, and stopped to talk to an older '50s Playmate, Delores Del Monte. He informed Delores that he came there looking for me and couldn't find me. She told him he wouldn't because I was blonde at the time and no one recognized me. She then escorted him to my table for an introduction.

I was touched and honored when the Navy Lt. presented me with the flag he was carrying. The flag had some of his top gun patches and pins from the war in Iraq attached to it. He told me that he and his brother David, who was a marine, loved my centerfold and it was their dream to meet me. I gave him some autographed photos and took a few with him.

Later I learned that his brother David died in Iraq. the Navy Lt. told me he was fixing up his brother's room with his desired autographed photo of me. This gesture truly touched my heart and showed me what an impact my photos had on such men.

They say that a picture is worth a thousand words, and I see now that this is so true. My photos inspired these soldiers to keep fighting for our country. This man fought his way back home to meet me, a dream he and his brother, who sadly didn't make it back, shared for a long time. Although his brother didn't make it back home, I could see his spirit in the Navy Lt.'s eyes as I signed a picture expressing how much I appreciated him.

This story especially made me proud to have been a pinup, and I wondered how many others have been inspired by my photos—stories that I may never hear.

You must keep your name in the public eye once you have made a recognized name for yourself. There are lots of charities, premiere parties, and openings to attend in Hollywood. Celebrity fashion shows are another venue in which to be seen by the press and have your name associated with other high-profile celebrities. Being seen and having your picture taken by the paparazzi is a great way to keep the image you want to create publicly and make it grow.

You must carefully pick the right events to attend for the greatest exposure. There are events such as the LA Mission that feed the homeless during Thanksgiving and Christmas. This is a great event for any celebrity to give of themselves, as well as get noticed with other high-profile celebrities for a great cause.

Sometimes it's good to let the public see that you are a real person, involved with real issues. Pinups are judged as fantasies, so it's great to show them who you are and what you passionately believe in. I am always open to give of myself to charities associated with child abuse. This is very personal to me, as I was sexually abused by my stepfather. Like Marilyn Monroe, I didn't know my real father and was also in foster homes. My success allows me to give back, and I choose to give to those children with whom I can relate.

I was once a "big sister" to a foster child at Hollygrove, which was the foster home that Marilyn Monroe used to be in. I found this to be very rewarding in my own healing process, and I'm grateful that I could make a difference in a child's life. I remember having a "big sister" when I was in a foster home who took me to my first movie. I had never been to a movie theater, and this was such a big deal to me. So it was my personal desire to find charities and events that I could participate in and that allowed me to give back in a positive manner.

A pinup has the means and the ability to make a lot of money and control her own images. This means she can use her images on products to market and sell to her ever-growing fan base, creating residual income to live on when she is old and gray.

Since pinup memorabilia is growing, I anticipate more future fans will be buying pinup collectibles. Posters, art, photos, T-shirts, coffee mugs, key chains, lighters, glasses, pens, lunch boxes, and mouse pads are just a few things that a pinup's image can be placed on for fans to collect. I have had my autograph and lip prints on wine glasses and beer mugs, trading cards, posters, and T-shirts.

Playboy now has its bunny logo on a line of clothing, lingerie, accessories for the home, and jewelry. There is even a Playboy store and a radio station exclusively devoted to its brand. There is no reason you too can't produce your own products with your image or logo. Just about anything you want to produce can be done with the technology that we have available today.

At age thirty-five, I entered cyberspace with my own Web site. I quickly learned that I needed some kind of product to reinvent myself. Since I had been out of the entertainment industry for several years, I was in dire need of something to promote myself. In addition, I'd just come out of a long-term relationship and needed to focus on something creative.

I decided to self-produce a Playboy-styled video about myself. I scouted the locations, hired makeup and hair people and photographers, and chose the original music I would use in the sixty-minute video. I saw that I had total control of me and my image. So I decided to produce, not only a DVD, but a book of recent pinup photos I owned. This project would be mine, and I would reintroduce the world to the pinup I had evolved into today. It was a way for me to show the different sides of my personality.

I starred in, directed, and even edited *Devin DeVasquez 2000* and *The Best of Devin DeVasquez*. The videos ran on pay-per-view and sold like hotcakes on my Web site. This was my reintroduction into pinup, since my last appearance was in the 1986 November issue of *Playboy*. I began to see that I could create anything I thought would sell.

It's best to start with products that won't be costly to produce, since it may be a while before you recoup your investment and make money from the item. Attend conventions that showcase new technologies and items that could help you grow your Internet business. It is also important to network with other people in the adult industry to learn how to promote your image. Pinup is the softest of what is considered *adult* in today's marketplace. Understanding the industry is important in marketing your brand.

I believe a pinup should educate herself in every area of the entertainment industry. Film, television, photography, fashion, music, art, and charity are all associated with pinup—thanks to Marilyn and Bettie, who pioneered the way. The world is her oyster and she can be whatever she wants to be.

Steps To Maximize Fame:

1. Attend autograph conventions; you can find these online. This is a great way to make industry contacts with other pinup models, photographers, and pinup artists.

2. Be seen at charity events and parties and have your picture taken by the paparazzi.

3. Shoot pictures with a variety of pinup photographers.

4. Agree to be painted by various pinup artists.

5. Get into an acting class and consult with others in the industry.

6. Create a variety of merchandise with your pinup image on it. Start with one or two items and build from there, such as T-shirts, coffee mugs, or key chains.

7. Create your own Web site and place your images on it so that you can correspond with fans. The average Web site isn't costly, but it does need to reflect your personality.

8. Do extra work in film and television to build contacts.

9. Be persistent and don't give up on your dream.

10. Be prepared for success and believe that your time to shine will come.

Dita Von Teese

Autographed headshot

Baby Dev Postcard

Best of Devin Cover

Bunny Devin

"Living in a Blonde World" book cover

Modeling photo

Chapter Four: Uniquely You

By now, you should understand that carving your own niche is important in making your brand stand out. The legends in pinup stand out from the rest because of their own unique style. We only have fifty years of pinup to draw on, and many of those legends are still alive today.

The pinup girls today could be legends of tomorrow, but it is up to them to make themselves unique, as well as to know and understand what their brand means to the public and how to keep it alive.

As previously mentioned, Dita Von Teese did this in spades and made a lucrative career from her love of the 1940s and '50s. She drew in an audience who had the same love of that era and wanted to find another fetish queen to crown. Dita made herself unique to her audience, yet she emulated poses of Bettie Page.

Perhaps you want to be another or more distinctive version of Rita Hayworth or Jayne Mansfield? Maybe your style is a combination of both or something totally unique in and of itself? Perhaps you have a love for the 1960s or 1970s and want to be the next Bo Derek? You don't have to be a centerfold to carve out an image for yourself, but you do have to have the desire to be glamorous and unique.

Some girls have it naturally, like Pamela Anderson, who just can't take a bad photo and oozes sex. It was no surprise that she became such a phenomenon and was often compared to Brigitte Bardot. Pam quickly carved her own niche with her larger-than-life image and her very public personal life.

Anna Nicole Smith is another pinup often compared to Marilyn Monroe, but she created her own personal outrageous image just by being herself. Her marriage to a much older billionaire and her battles with her weight made her a much-talked-about celebrity, which led to her own reality TV series.

Just thinking about Dita, Pam, or Anna Nicole brings to mind a certain type of image that these women have engraved into our minds. All of these women are no doubt beautiful but very different from each other. Their names are distinguished, and their photos evoke a certain fantasy or opinion about them, based on how they have chosen to brand themselves. All are unique and successful in their own right; and all will be remembered for years to come.

Although you don't have to be a centerfold to be a pinup girl, the association with *Playboy* gives you credibility in this industry. Just about all the famous pinups have been associated in some way with *Playboy*. The Internet has given the pinup industry more of a playing field, but *Playboy* is still the grandfather of the pinup world and always will be.

So how do you become a Playboy Playmate? Many girls send in photos taken by either a professional photographer or their husband or boyfriend. The photos should show how you photograph, so a good headshot is a must. A full-length shot of your body should show your curves and a good shot of your breasts. Once the photos are sent into *Playboy*, they are reviewed by a photo editor. You are sent a letter if they are interested in testing you with more professional photos, from which they will make their decision.

The process is tedious, as so many girls these days send in their photos. Once you are accepted, test photos are done with hair and makeup in a *Playboy* setting to see if you make the cut. If the editors like what they see, a centerfold shoot is scheduled. It usually takes a week to shoot. The centerfold shoot is shot with an 8x10-view camera, and the model must be very still and do the exact same pose over and over again, until they get the perfect centerfold.

If you are lucky enough to make it this far and a centerfold is shot, there is still a waiting process. Hugh Hefner must decide if he likes the centerfold. I've known some girls who have waited up to two years to find out if their centerfold was approved! If it is, you are given a month and the "small camera" photos are shot. These are the rest of the photos that would go with your pictorial story in the magazine.

The process is nerve-racking. By the time a Playboy Playmate becomes a fantasy girl of the month, she has been photographed thousands of times by a *Playboy* photographer to get the best photos.

I have known girls who have tested and been rejected by Playboy, only to try again and make it. So if this is your dream, don't give up on it. When I decided I wanted to be a Playmate, my look was a rarity. There were so many blondes dominating the magazine that my chances seemed slim to none, but I was confident and determined.

Even if you are not a Playmate, there are other ways to be a part of Playboy to give you a jump start on your pinup career—for instance, the Playboy Lingerie magazines and the Playboy Cyber Girls, as well as the Playboy Channel. There are more opportunities now than ever to be a part of their brand.

You may have a love for leather and lace, or feathers and boas. Maybe high heels and stockings or lingerie and corsets make you feel sexy? Whatever makes you feel sexy, glamorous, and distinct play with it. Take photos in your favorite outfits and see what develops. Everyone has something unique and special about them. You have to find out what that is for you and play it up. Don't be afraid to show off who you are. The inner confidence must come out above everything else, because that truly is what is sexy.

Marilyn Monroe created her own persona. She came up with her name, breathy voice, and seductive walk to stand out from all the other blondes. There was no one like her, and the public couldn't get enough. She played the dumb blonde so well that many people thought that was her true character. It became a blessing and a curse for her to deal with in her career. Marilyn was, in fact, a smart and excellent actress whom many people didn't get to know. She was in control of her image and of how she wanted the public to view her.

Plastic surgery is also sometimes necessary for a pinup to attain her desired form, and there are many who have no problems admitting to such surgeries. Marilyn had a nose job, as did I. Pamela Anderson and Anna Nicole had their breasts enlarged by surgery. Many girls have gone under the knife to improve themselves physically. Pretty much anything you'd want to change or improve can be achieved with plastic surgery. There are even reality shows devoted to plastic surgery.

Some beauties have an inner quality that exceeds their outer appearance. We might think that her physical look is in need of something extra, say, her breasts are a little too small. Perhaps a nose job would soften her look or make it stronger and more photogenic? Whatever the reason, not all pinups are perfect. Pretty much all of them have had a little fine-tuning in some department.

Whatever you can do to make your own uniqueness stand out, do it. This is all part of creating the pinup girl you wish to be. The pinup girl is constantly evolving, so it's hard to say who she is exactly, but one can see that she is unique, and because of this; it's hard to stop watching her every move. The distinct qualities will keep you interesting, and thus keep the public wanting more of you.

Once your uniqueness is defined, it's easier to play it up and re-emphasize it. Marilyn's voice, Dita's corsets, Pam's outrageous clothing, Bettie's famous bangs, and Anna Nicole's tattoos—these are the things that these pinups have engraved into our minds. The mere thought of a breathy voice reminds you of Marilyn. Anyone wearing Bettie's bangs is thought fashionable. Pam now has her own clothing line, and Dita made corsets popular again.

Think of pinup as the merging of fashion and lingerie into one. Define what your look needs in the way of fashion to make it sexy. Look at it in terms of clothing, hair and makeup, and projected personality. In other words, make the image you are creating suit the clothing, hair, and makeup, and fit it into whatever type of personality you are developing.

Remember, pinup is fantasy, or at least part fantasy, so have fun with it. Feel good about who you are and what you are projecting. Live it and love living it, because that is what will sell your image and make you stand out.

At forty-five, Devin DeVasquez is still evolving. I love playing with different looks, hairstyles, and fashion. Many of my fans love to see what I'll wear to an event, and the paparazzi love to photograph me. I find that my image fits what I've tried to project—one of class and seductive allure, mixed with the self-assurance that comes with age, which makes for one hell of a woman, baby!

The pinup girl is all woman, and she loves being a woman and all that it entails. Every woman has her own wonderful uniqueness that makes her special. It's not just how she looks physically. She must possess something of an intangible quality about her personality. Her eyes speak an unspoken language that you long to hear. Her lips want to say things you can't understand. Her body says yes to any fantasy you may have. Her photo is worth a thousand words that are not needed, and her presence is magical. This is the type of uniqueness to strive for, even if it seems unbelievable.

A clear vision of what you want to project is important in finding your own uniqueness. I understood that my exotic, natural child-woman demeanor, mixed with a seductive allure, gave me an advantage that few pinups had.

Women want to know my beauty secrets, and men of all ages still find me lustful. There are not too many other pinups in my age range who have my career. This gives me the opportunity to reinvent my image, which is constantly evolving.

The pinup girl is larger than life, and the more you make your unique qualities stand out, the more visible you will become. The evolution of what is created from that unique quality remains to be seen, for beauty is in the eye of the beholder. What I hope comes to mind is an image of empowerment and strength, as well as seduction and natural beauty.

The public will respond to your unique qualities, and from this you will know and understand what it means. It is important to understand your own unique qualities and perfect them. If you are passionate about showing them off, everyone will respond to them; they will demand attention.

Julie Strain is a perfect example of a unique pinup. Julie was "Penthouse Pet of the Year" and made a name for herself by doing B movies. Julie stands over six feet tall and appears to be a larger-than-life person. She became a cult phenomenon in *Heavy Metal* magazine and even had a *Heavy Metal* movie dedicated to her unbelievable image.

Julie's love for beautiful pinup models made her a natural behind the camera as a photographer. She loves to imitate Bettie Page and Marilyn Monroe, among others. Her diversity in front of the camera is truly amazing. She has self-published books with tons of images of herself in all her pinup glory. Julie should have been a super fashion model, but her superb physique had pinup icon written all over it. She has been an inspiration to me and encouraged me to produce *Devin DeVasquez 2000*, as well as my own photo book with her photography, *Living In A Blonde World*. She gave her love of pinup to the world for their enjoyment.

Julie loves nothing more than to produce a variety of collectible products with her images. She has produced trading cards, books, art, dolls, calendars, and action figures. Her fan base grows daily, and it's obvious that Julie is a legend in the making.

I learned a lot from Julie about cultivating my own image as a pinup. She introduced me to pinup artist Olivia, who has done several paintings of each of us. Olivia has also done a multitude of paintings of Dita and Pamela Anderson. I understood from Julie the importance of having such an admired pinup artist paint us. Since Playboy introduced us to Vargas and Nagel, artists such as Olivia will be revered as future legendary pinup artists.

Julie's association with such artists and photographers helped her get amazing pinup images of herself out publicly. Julie has also produced, directed, taught classes, wrote magazine columns, and bred other pinups to follow in her footsteps. She is one of the most unique pinups of our time, and there will never be another Julie, that's for sure! The fact that her best friend is pinup legend Mamie Van Doren speaks volumes. The notes they compare are interesting indeed. I have learned quite a bit from both of these ladies, and I'm grateful for having known them.

Mamie is still a glamorous babe today and stands out in a crowd as one seductive grandmother. I read her book *Playing the Field* and interviewed her for my Web site. I learned a lot of the history of Hollywood.

Mamie followed Jayne Mansfield into the movie industry in the '60s, creating comparisons between the two of them. She educated me a little about Marilyn's last days in Hollywood and about their friendship. She told me how sad Marilyn seemed the last time she saw her and gave me insight on how tough it was to be a strong, sexy woman in her era.

The politics, the sex scandals, and Mamie's sexual encounters with Hollywood's sexiest men (she knew them all) created great stories for her to share. I soaked in everything that she told me and found her to be strong, diverse, and an extremely talented lady. She was a true actress on screen and on stage, and she had a fabulous life with amazing men. Julie and Mamie are two peas in a pod today, and it's easy to see why.

I remember hearing stories about Julie Strain even before I met her. I was a little intimidated when I first met her but quickly found her to be really down to earth. Julie and I both love to cook, and she can make the most amazing chili! I loved going to visit her just to eat.

The pinup world is never boring, and the stories that emerge about today's pinup stars help keep the mystique interesting. I've been told silly and crazy stories about myself and found them to be very funny. It's the uniqueness of the pinup that drives people to gossip about them. Can you imagine the Anna Nicole Smith stories that will develop over the years?

I think it's easy to grasp what is distinct about the previously mentioned pinups. They all have their own image that grows daily into its own unique entity. It's apparent to see that Julie's merchandising abilities will make her image bigger with each passing year. Mamie gave us the insight to see the potential of tomorrow's pinup queen. Dita carved a look that is retro movie star and married the most bizarre rock star of our time. Pamela Anderson is still wowing the world in every area of the media.

These women are showing us how powerful the pinup girl has become. Learning from them is essential in becoming the best pinup you can possibly be. Since I know all of them, it was easy for me to admire and emulate some of their talents. I understand the importance of standing out and making your own uniqueness stand on its own.

Finding Your Own Uniqueness:

1. You can borrow from past pinups, but let your own uniqueness shine.

2. Consult with professional hair and makeup artists if you need help.

3. Play up your strengths—maybe it's your personality, hair, body, or face. Seldom do we have it all.

4. Don't be discouraged if you want it as a career. It takes time and effort like anything.

5. Study poses from past pinups and perfect your own.

6. Shoot a lot of pictures to perfect your modeling skills.

Playboy cover

Devin finds a quiet moment to enjoy the feel of the warm Hawaiian sun on her back as she explores the countryside.

Ujena Ad

Swimwear photo

Photo from "Living in a Blonde World"

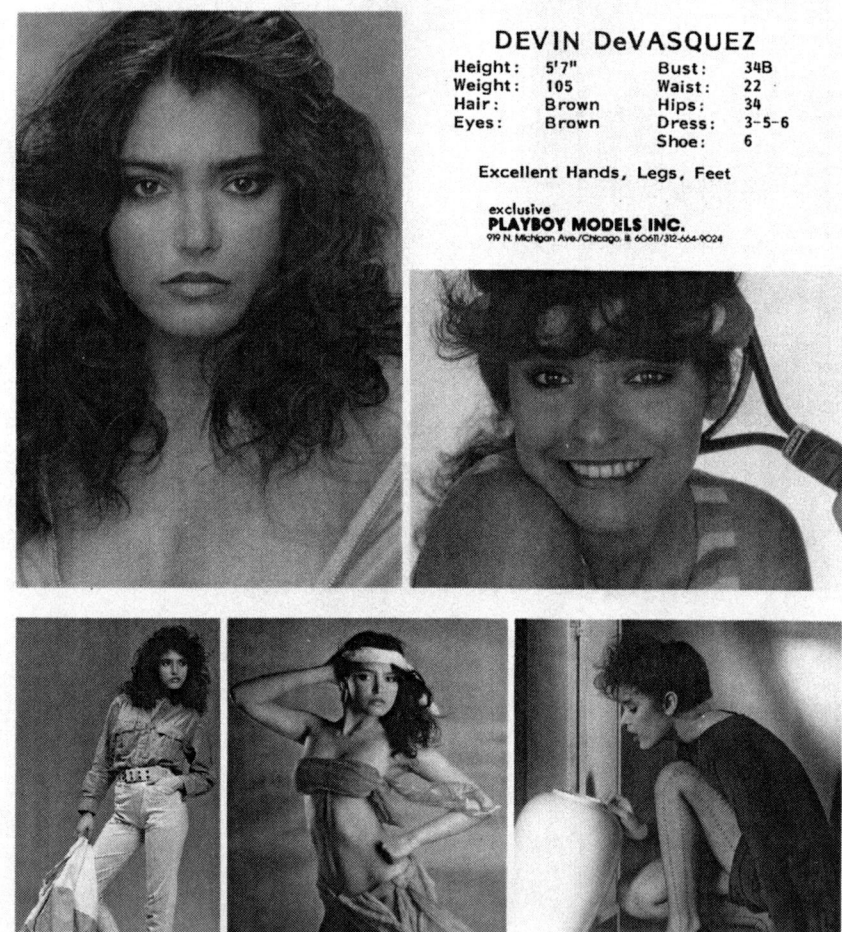

1st Modeling zed card

MODEL MANAGEMENT
John Casablancas
9255 Sunset Blvd., Suite 1125, Los Angeles, CA 90069 Tel: (213) 274 9395 Telex: 194967

Elite Zed Card

Modeling photo

Zed Card back

Devin Devasquez

Trashy Model Agency
402 N. La Cienega Blvd.
Los Angeles, California 90048
Tel: 310.659.7225 • Fax 310.652.9567

Zed Card front

Modeling photo

Ujena cover

Chapter Five:
The Internet and Publicity

The Internet is a powerful and effective tool for a home-based business, and just about everyone has a computer today. The Internet has changed the way we communicate; it enables us to see and hear the people we communicate with all over the world! This new technology has made the world a much smaller place.

It's a proven fact that anyone can promote themselves and even make money from the Internet. It seems anyone who is anyone has a Web site and is marketing something through this new media. It is also apparent that television fuels a Web site. Web sites need advertising, and as we know, television is a good medium through which to sell and market products and services.

The world is at your fingertips, and you are in control of it. Everyone has the chance to become a star and get his or her fifteen minutes of fame and fortune. It is a new and open playing field. We can promote and market anything with e-mail and get the information out to millions of people in an instant. Sounds amazing, doesn't it?

The Internet has also changed the way we view pinups, and new cyber stars are born every day. This was my inspiration for a documentary I'm currently working on, in which I personally interviewed legend Bettie Page and Dita Von Teese, along with top pinup artists and photographers. I saw that through the Internet future pinups could take on a whole new powerful position as never before in history.

Bettie became bigger than life before my very eyes. Her popularity grew at a rapid pace, she became a living legend, and I had the privilege to get to know her. This gift inspired me to want to become the best pinup I could. Perhaps I could be a fraction of what Bettie was, and still is, someday in the future?

I also knew some of the first Internet stars personally, such as Cindy Margolis. Cindy was known as the "most downloaded woman of the Internet." However, Cindy was a swimsuit poster girl and never posed nude. Most of her fans were young boys not old enough to even look at *Playboy*.

I watched Cindy market her Web site as a place to communicate with her "cyber buddies," as she called them. Since she was such a homebody, this was perfect for my pal Cindy. She could stay home and answer e-mail. The more e-mails she answered, the larger her fan base grew.

Soon she hired a publicist to get her on television shows like *EXTRA* to promote her calendars and posters, as well as her Web site. She discovered that every time she appeared on television, her Web site traffic went through the roof and tons more fans found out about her. Cindy's appearance on television shows promised that the ratings would skyrocket. Cindy would e-mail her growing fan base, and they would watch her shows, thus causing ratings to surge. Cindy was smart enough to take this further and made use of magazine media as well.

Eventually, she was offered her own show on CBS, on which I proudly made a guest appearance. However, the network didn't quite understand this new Internet media. They put her in lingerie in front of a South Beach audience to promote kids having fun on the beach. Little did they realize that Cindy's audience couldn't drink the beer that sponsored commercials for Cindy's show. The audience most hit shows want are ages eighteen to thirty-five who have money to spend. Cindy's show was canceled after only one season. However, her regular appearances on *Howard Stern* kept her Web site thriving, though it never made her a dime. The deals and connections she made through promoting it made her tons and gave her a title in the *Guinness Book*.

Cindy later took a break to get married and start a family. After a struggle to get pregnant, Cindy had a beautiful baby boy and could now enjoy staying home for a while, which was her favorite thing to do. Cindy even incorporated her pregnancy into her Web site. The images and the Web site itself continue to change, along with Cindy and her career. She is a marketing icon and has self-promoted her image to perfection. I learned so much just watching her, and I admire her greatly as a businesswoman and a friend.

I also interviewed the woman who challenged Cindy's title as the most downloaded woman in cyberspace. Danni Ash is a former stripper turned multimillion-dollar businesswoman. Danni's interview was very insightful and intriguing, not to mention informative about the Internet. Danni marketed herself from a small apartment, while stripping in Las Vegas. She was even arrested while stripping in a nightclub, which led to her decision to focus on her Web site.

She used her natural double D breasts to make her millions with her Web site, www.danni.com. Hundreds of other busty beautiful models were featured on Danni's site in photos, videos, and live chats 24/7. It's the largest strip club in the world. Thousands of members pay $19.95 a month to view thousands of photos and hours of video footage on their favorite pinups.

Because Danni's site is so large and there is so much to see there, the downloads were numerous. She too is in the *Guinness Book* and claims to now have more downloads than Cindy. A huge battle over it was discussed on *Howard Stern* with Danni; Cindy refused to appear on the show to comment.

Unlike Cindy, Danni makes millions off of her Web site. She sells products and produces her own content in photo shoots and video productions and is quoted to have said that she is a "publicity whore." She understands that publicity fuels that site and helps to make it so profitable.

Danni also set the standard on how to produce a good adult Web site. I have followed her lead with my own Web site; everything from hosting the site on a good server to how to obtain a merchant account to marketing your image, I discovered from my association with Danni.

As you can see, Danni and Cindy used the Internet as a useful marketing tool to promote themselves and their products. They were pioneers of the Internet, and I got to see firsthand how they used their Web sites to their advantage.

There are so many more Web sites out in cyberspace today, so the market is saturated with them. That's why it's necessary to understand how and what you want to promote before embarking on the venture. Knowledge is power, and the more you understand the Internet, the more useful it can be for you as a pinup.

Television appearances send tons of traffic to a Web site, and this traffic produces paying customers. It seems everyone on television now has a Web site to go to for more information about their show. The hit TV show *American Idol* allowed the television audience to determine the winner of the singing competition, and it in turn made millions off of the new idols. They understood that if the public voted and liked a certain contestant, then they would be more likely to buy their albums.

The Internet and the television set go hand in hand today. The Internet allows the viewers to interact with their television sets. This has changed the way we forever view things, because we can not only view them but interact directly with some of them.

I found that out from my own Web site, www.devindevasquez.com, for my fans loved the chats I had with them. I could be seen in a chat room by several people at once. They would type questions to me, and I'd answer them while they were viewing me. I had sound at one point that enabled them to hear me as well.

The future is now with the technology that is on hand today. The technology is also constantly changing and rapidly growing to an astounding level of communication. This enables us to have access to massive numbers of people, which is tremendous for the purpose of marketing.

It is strange to think back twenty years to the time when I was a Playboy Playmate. Men could only look at my photos in hopes that they may meet me someday. In many cases, I'm sure I wasn't even a reality, for there was only a picture to dream about. Now we have chats in which that person in the photo speaks to the admirer. Just think how different it might have been for fans of Marilyn or Bettie if they had had this technology to communicate with them in their prime.

I have communicated over the phone with fans all over the world via another interesting Web site, www.keen.com. These fans pay a set fee of $3.99 a minute to speak with their favorite starlet or pinup. They can ask questions or find out where her next personal appearance will be in their area. They form a long and sometimes intimate friendship with some, and simply have sexy, fun conversation with others.

I have found that fans of a pinup are very loyal to their queen. Some may fantasize about you for years and happily follow your legacy and support your success. Many of my own fans have shown such devotion. I receive wonderful cards on my birthday, Valentine's Day, and Christmas. They collect a lot of my memorabilia, such as photos, clothing items, and DVDs. They enter dating contests and have bidding wars over personal items I auction.

I can let them view me at home, and I even run my entire business from my home. I make a living being Devin DeVasquez, which is a wonderful way to earn a living. Fans seem to relish paying to join my Web site, to buy my photos and personal items, to visit me at personal appearances and pay for photos with me. They eagerly buy any kind of merchandise I choose to market with my image on it.

There are major collectors of pinup art, and pinup artists such as Olivia, Walter Girotto, Michael Mobius, and Jon Hul have painted my image several times for future generations to admire. This is the ultimate for a pinup. Having your image painted by such pinup artists is quite an honor, and a prestigious one at that.

The Internet has enabled several money-making venues. Anything you wish to sell can be sold on your Web site. You are in total control of marketing and making a profit from your own images.

Playboy even started to lose control over the world of pinup, which it fathered. Hefner did not understand the Internet in the early days of its conception. A lawsuit involving Playboy and Playmate of the Year Terri Wells made history. Terri was sued because she was the first Playmate to have an adult Web site with paying customers. She used her title of "Playmate of the Year" to promote herself. Playboy felt this was an infringement on its copyright, since the given title belonged to Playboy. It also claimed that her images were not suitable for a Playboy Playmate, as they were a little more risqué.

Terri in turn rebutted with claims that it was a control issue of Hugh Hefner, with whom she had a sexual affair during her Playmate reign. She was asked to take down her Web site and refused.

The court battle was costly for both sides, but a ruling in Terri's favor allowing her to use her title gave all Playboy Playmates that same right. This was a great victory in favor of any celebrity wanting to use any title he or she may have won in order to promote himself or herself for profit. This win changed everything that cyberspace was becoming, and Playboy had no choice but to embrace the fact that former Playmates could do as they wished, in regards to their images after their Playboy days were over.

One former Playmate of the month, Teri Weigel, went on to become the first Playmate to attain adult stardom in hardcore porn. Playboy disowned and banned her, claiming she was unfit to be a Playmate. However, Hefner was always quoted as saying, "Once a Playmate, always a Playmate," a title that remains with you for the rest of your life. It's a title that is life changing and always will be.

Two other Playmates went on to pose for *Penthouse* and made history as both Playmates and "Pets of the Month." Still, those girls had a loyal fan base, and they continued to brand their images, no matter what Playboy thought. The Internet proved to be extremely powerful in marketing and branding their images, helping them to thrive beyond Playboy.

The world was changing rapidly before my eyes, and I had no choice but to change with it. In making choices in my own career, I often had to be careful not to cross the line; I want to maintain my image as something I can always be comfortable with and proud of. I'm constantly making decisions about what projects I'll work on and people I want to work with. These decisions are crucial and will take me beyond who I am today.

Publicity is a great way to help your Web site thrive. Publicists can be quite expensive, for they understand how much publicity is worth to most celebrities. Celebrities go on television talk shows to promote their movies and television shows and to make personal endorsements. Cyber stars of the Internet can now hire a publicist to promote their Web sites. The more familiar an audience is with that site, the more traffic is driven to that Web site and thus the greater potential for money.

Jenna Jameson, a former well-known porn star, is a perfect example of a self-made mogul. She used her Web site to make herself one of the most recognized and respected porn stars. Jenna eventually crossed over to mainstream television and now produces her own products. She had full control over her brand and everything associated with her brand. Jenna wrote a book on her life as a porn star and has made millions being Jenna Jameson.

You are in control of your Web site. The content you provide is up to your discretion. But keep in mind that the money you spend to promote your Web site is essential to helping keep it alive. You can have the best Web site out there, but if no one knows about it, then what good is it?

Magazine appearances are another essential for maintaining and elevating the status of a pinup. A new model on the scene could become a star in the pinup world with regular magazine appearances. There are lots of men's print magazines on the market as well as online magazines; and they are constantly looking for the next hot girl to discover.

Online interviews are another way to publicize your name and brand. There are many online magazines looking for a new Web site to talk about. Linking yourself to as many online magazines and other adult sites as you can is mandatory for getting noticed. A good marketing plan and Web master are essential. Since there is so much competition today on the Web with so many sites popping up daily, you must constantly stay on top of what's new and hot now.

Video chats are a great way to grow your fan base. Cam shows are extremely popular, since the fans can see you and chat with you at the same time. There are ways to make them private and one on one, which is even better and more exclusive to that fan. People are willing to pay a premium price by the minute for this service.

If you have a successful Web site that is making pretty good money, it is probably a good idea to invest in a publicist. A publicist can get you in magazines, on talk shows, and into celebrity events, thus keeping your name and image in the public eye.

I suggest interviewing several different publicists and asking questions such as who they represent and what connections they have to what magazines and media. These questions will help you determine the publicist that will best suit your needs. You need to be careful, however, not to pick the wrong publicist.

I once hired a high-profile publicist after my win on *Star Search*. She represented several well-known actresses on television shows at that time. She also seemed very well connected to the types of magazines and media that I wanted to be a part of.

She was also very expensive and wanted me to have professional publicity photos taken with a high-profile and expensive photographer. I was naive to all of this and agreed. I spent so much money and got very little publicity from her representation. Seems she was way too busy with her higher-profile clients to spend the necessary time on me. This is what you must be careful of when choosing a publicist. Some of them talk a good game to get your money and then do nothing for you.

I could have probably gone with a smaller, lesser known publicist who would have really worked for me. It's a hard decision to make, because there are no sure bets that you will get what you pay for.

I suggest getting to know media people personally through party events. Because pinup girls are always welcome at parties, this should come about easily. There are many magazine parties, charity events, film premieres, and club or restaurant openings to attend in Hollywood every day. Going to these events is a great way to make connections and promote what you are doing, as well as be seen. Looking your best and getting photographed at these events can also provide content to post on your Web site.

Many celebrities attend these kinds of events, and there is usually paparazzi present on the "red carpet." Getting to know the paparazzi, and letting them get to know you, is a great way to make some of the media work for you.

I sometimes throw parties and invite celebrities and paparazzi to attend. This keeps my name buzzing about town, and I get free pictures of my party if I give an exclusive to one photographer. I have built a relationship over the years with certain paparazzi photographers, and they happily come to my events for an exclusive.

When you are a pinup girl, building relationships with a variety of photographers is essential to your business. Photographers love to photograph beautiful women, and having several on hand can be of benefit, depending on what your needs are at the time. I have a list of fashion photographers, glamour photographers, portrait photographers, pinup photographers, and paparazzi photographers on hand for any given photo need.

When you have a Web site, it must be supplied with content that you produce. Remember, a pinup girl is glamorous, sexy, and always being photographed. If you have a list of photographers, you must also have a list of makeup artists on hand. A good makeup artist is needed for celebrity events and shoots. Sometimes a good stylist is necessary, but most pinup girls create their own style.

Dita did that with corsets. She had hundreds of custom-made corsets and lived in them. Soon fans tried to copy her style, and corsets became popular thanks to Dita. The pinup girl sets trends for others to follow; she marches to her own beat and makes her own rules. Just thinking of her name brings to mind a larger-than-life image of glamour and beauty.

The power of the Internet is growing daily and, by extension, the power of the pinup. Understanding this new and rapidly growing entity is mandatory. You must keep your fans happy and supply them with new collectible items of your image. I know many pinups who have thousands of never-released photos that they are saving for future products. So even after they retire, there is still merchandise to feed the public's craving for their queens.

Julie Strain was smart enough to see this in pinup models. She took up photography and began to shoot photographs of each and every beautiful and up-and-coming pinup on the scene today. She plastered them on her mega hit Web site and her fans can't get enough. Because Julie owns the copyrights of these photos, she will be able to produce merchandise for years to come. Julie used the Internet to launch her photography career and keep her name and image in the public eye. Her site generates money, a growing fan base, merchandise, and her own self-produced images and videos. Julie's Web site will be worth so much more in the future; its growth has already been remarkable in just the past few years.

Technology is making it possible to really get to know the fantasy girls of the past and present. The Internet allows you to get more of an insight of her personality and interact with her privately through Web cams.

The pinup has more avenues in which to make money from her nude images. She is in control and driving her career with her own bold, unique qualities. The pinup girl is a star in the making, and the Internet is her stage.

Two of the biggest Internet sites, www.myspace.com and www.ebay.com, have over two hundred million viewers to whom one can market merchandise and promote themselves.

Playboy is one of eBay's biggest sellers, and most of the Playmates along with countless other hotties are splashed all over MySpace with their own pages to promote themselves.

I personally sell old photos, new photos, and swimwear and lingerie directly to fans on a daily basis. It seems they can't get enough. There are fans who collect trading cards, photos, lingerie, swimsuits, and just about anything else you can think of on eBay.

If you are going to start a business on eBay, you must first have a PayPal account. It's an easy and safe way for most people to conduct transactions over the Internet. You must have a checking account to start a PayPal account. Then go to www.paypal.com and sign up for it.

Once you are in business on eBay, you can find just about anything imaginable online and buy or sell it. I bought the first issue of *Playboy* with Marilyn Monroe on the cover for $3000! There were fifteen other people bidding for it, and I was so happy and nervous during the last few minutes of that auction. Such auctions are fun and addictive.

You can now give your fans a piece of you to take home with them and get as creative as you wish in the world's biggest shopping mall. There are also other auction sites that are adult-oriented in content, on which a pinup can sell provocative photos, DVDs, lingerie, and other personal items. Paypal can now be used on these sites along with cashier's checks and money orders.

A well-known pinup star can earn several hundreds of dollars a day from auction items alone. I sold the bra and panty set I wore on *Married with Children* for $750!

It's best to start an auction at a low price and put a reserve price on the item (what you will sell the item for); in that way, you have a better chance at increasing the bid well over the reserve price. You may also post an item at a "Buy It Now" price and sell it outright.

It is also important to direct as many people as you can to your Web site to purchase merchandise directly from your store because most auction sites charge fees to sell your items and final fees based on what you sell your item for. However, keeping your profile and image on as many sites as possible is what it is all about. Your fan base will be loyal to you if you take the time to communicate effectively, offer good products, and provide timely and effective service.

It's never been more profitable to have a business right out of the privacy of your own home, and the sky is the limit. A pinup model has many ways to make money and increase her popularity on the Internet. Auction sites are just one avenue. Your image is in your control, and you can have it be whatever you wish today. The pinup girl is here to stay, and she's also a smart, savvy businesswoman who is in control of her destiny!

Millions of Web sites are popping up every day, and there are new and interesting pinups to view on a daily basis. The average housewife in middle America can become a pinup model if she so desires. The possibility of your wildest dreams coming true is there for the taking, and the whole world will be watching and admiring your own unique beauty. Dream big, because these dreams can come true.

Important Things To Know About Building Your Web Site:

1. You must register your name, whether it's your real name or a made-up one, and own it. You can go to www.networksolutions.com to do this.

2. Find a good Web master. One who is a fan is always great, but if you hire someone, make sure you pay them a fee to maintain your Web site.

3. You must find a good Web designer to design your site. You can use the same person to be your Web master, but it's best to keep them separate in my opinion.

4. Use your resources to network at conventions, perhaps throw a party every once in a while to collaborate with well-known photographers, models, and artists. This provides great content for your Web site.

5. Investigate publicists; they can be costly and sometimes do nothing much for you.

6. Allow enough money for at least a year to kick off your Internet venture. If you can get investors who believe in you and your star quality to help, that's wonderful. When starting out, like any business, it takes a while to generate profits. Remember, you are building on who you are and that is an intangible thing.

7. Try to get invited to celebrity events as much as possible, such as premieres and charities. A publicist can help with this, but also contacts within the industry help a lot. This is why networking is essential.

8. Set up your own merchant account for online sales from your Web site. This can be costly but most effective in controlling your brand and your money.

9. Produce products to promote yourself on your Web site and make money. Start small and build from there.

10. Join chat rooms and spread the word about who you are with fans.

Steps To Successful Auctions:

Research your market and create good, quality merchandise to sell.

Follow the rules pertaining to each auction site on which you sell.

Create good communication with your buyers.

Find your niche. Remember, there's room for everyone!

Dream big and think positive!

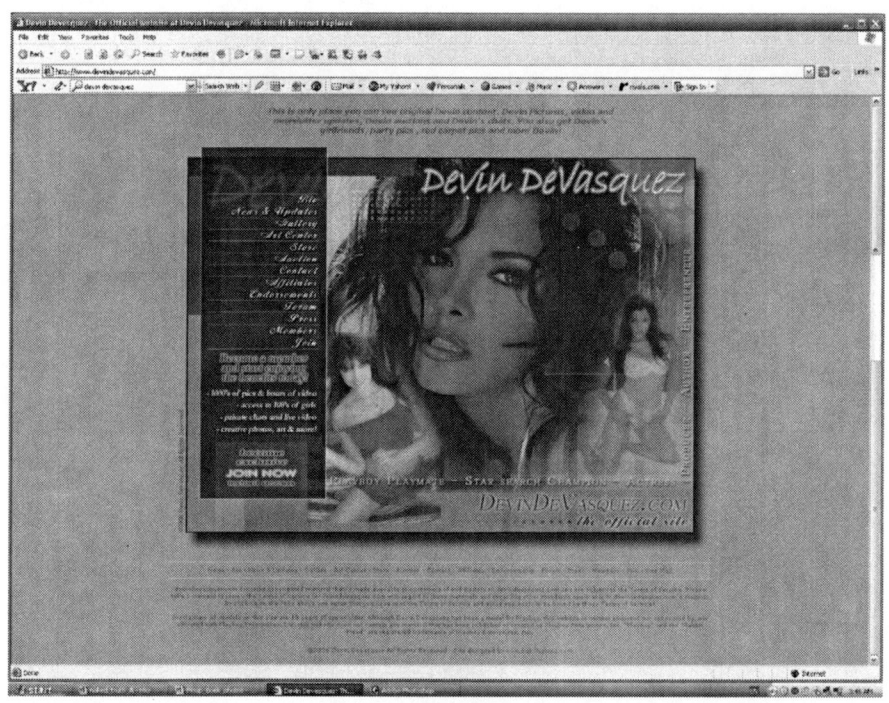

My Website

Cindy Margolis

Julie Strain

Julie Strain

Julie Strain

Julie Strain

Olivia Card Painting

Olivia Card Painting

Chapter Six: Personal Appearances

Just as television appearances send tons of traffic to your Web site—in turn giving you paying customers—personal appearances connect you to your fan base and keep them loyal to you. Your fans want to know who you really are and how they can meet you.

Personal appearances allow fans to meet and greet you in the flesh. They can get their picture taken with you and buy autographed merchandise for their ongoing collections. There is no bigger thrill than to express themselves to you in person.

I have fans who are like groupies; they bring me flowers, candy, and tokens of their affection. Many of them just want to hang out and watch my every move or talk. They will buy anything just to keep the conversation going. Over the years, I have developed nice friendships with some. In turn, I am always trying to think of ways to make them happy. For instance, I have had a "win a date" contest and auctions on my Web site exclusively for my members.

It is important to understand what to do at personal appearances. I try to have a new product out every year, such as a DVD, calendar, book, or art piece on display. It is also important to have business cards with your photo and Web site on them for fans to take home. Many fans will go to your Web site and buy something online later.

Appearances are also great for networking with other models, photographers, and collectors. There are many comic book shows across the country to participate in. Some shows are specialty conventions devoted to a specific type of fan. Many pinups are welcome to sign autographs at these shows; however, it is important to understand your fan base and what they are looking for from you.

A Web site helps you see where your particular fans are located, and this helps you decide what region of the country you should visit for the best results. There's no point in traveling to a show in the Midwest if most of your fans are coming from the South.

As a pinup builds her name and recognition, her fan base will increase, thus increasing her sales of merchandise. Many pinups have had careers in film and television, such as Stella Stevens and Mamie Van Doren. These women still do autograph shows.

Autograph shows now cater to just about every type of fan. I have come across many interesting opportunities from autograph shows. Sometimes film and television producers seek out their next starlet at these shows. I have been offered jobs in film, photography, and art through appearances.

It's always interesting to walk around some of the sci-fi conventions and see the various products that are on the market and the people promoting them. There are still tons of fans collecting *Star Wars* products. You'd be surprised at the diehard fans who dress up as their favorite sci-fi characters and go to these shows.

There are shows devoted to horror, pinup, sci-fi, and fetish, which all welcome pinups. You can usually make some pretty good cash at a weekend convention. Press and documentary makers also frequent these shows and the celebrity signings.

It is important to have a good demeanor when doing personal appearances. I have seen well-known celebrities appear grumpy, as if they didn't want to be there, which can have a lasting effect on a devoted fan.

I always try to strike up conversations with fans to let them know I care. You never know what interesting connection you may make from these encounters. It's important to have fun!

I have made some terrific friends at these shows. One such friend is Sandra Taylor. Sandra Taylor, formerly a Penthouse Pet, became a Playboy cover girl when she starred in a Steven Segal film and appeared regularly on *Howard Stern*. Sandra also kept her name in the public eye through cameos in director Garry Marshall's films. She is a big draw at autograph shows because she has diversified herself so much, despite being a dedicated mother of two and a housewife. Sandra keeps up her pinup image with Olivia paintings and cross country personal appearances that keep her fans happy.

I personally like doing appearances; I just don't care for the pains of traveling these days and prefer doing them close to my home in Los Angeles. A pinup can now attend and sign autographs at most all conventions. These appearances can result in thousands of dollars, as well as publicity with her fan base and the chance to work with others in the industry.

Below is a list of a few well-known conventions that a pinup can attend. You can search the Internet for many more around the country and the world under "comic conventions."

- GLAMOURCON is a pinup convention that enables mostly pinup collectors and fans to meet a vast number of pinups at the same show. Held two to four times a year, this convention has been showcasing pinups from the past five decades for over ten years.

- THE HOLLYWOOD COLLECTOR'S SHOW enables fans of old TV personalities to gather, get autographs, and chat and take pictures with their favorite celebrities. Playmates who have appeared in television and films can now participate in the show, held four times a year in Los Angeles and Chicago.

- THE CHILLER THEATER is a large East Coast convention, held twice a year in New Jersey for fans of horror films and their celebrities.

- THE COMIC CON CONVENTION is the largest comic book and science fiction convention in the world. It is held once a year in San Diego and hosts over 63,000 fans, allowing them to meet comic artists, celebrities, and favorite television and film characters.

- WIZARD WORLD is a comic show held in Chicago, Philadelphia, and Atlanta yearly.

My ex-husband Randy, Devin, and Hugh Hefner

Above: Devin and Renee Tenison
Below: Ex-husband Randy, Devin, Pam Anderson, and Scott Baio

Above: Devin and Apollonia
Below: Mamie Van Doren and Devin

Noel Blanc, Devin, and Tony Curtis

Devin and Ed O'Neil

Christina Applegate and Devin

Devin and Bill Maher

Blonde Devin

Blonde Devin

Modeling photo

Modeling photo

Modeling photo

Modeling photo

Modeling photo

Apollonia, Carmen Electra, Devin

Devin and James Caan

Devin and Mick Jagger

Dita Von Teese and Devin

Hugh Hefner and Devin

Victoria Silvstedt and Devin

Chapter Seven: Steps To Stardom

Posing nude changes your life forever, and the transition into film and television is very common for centerfolds. Stars like Pamela Anderson and Anna Nicole Smith made it typical for today's pinup. However, there are specific steps to take in making the transition and being prepared for stardom.

In the early years of pinup, modeling was the most a pinup girl could hope to achieve, and most girls used a different name for mainstream modeling. There were exceptions, of course, but very few. Pinup modeling was a special kind of modeling and limited to few girls who chose to do it.

Few pinups made the transition into film and television, and if they did, it was limited to sexy roles and bit parts. The addition of cable and home videos enabled change and offered more opportunities for pinups.

Still, it was hard for Hollywood to view the pinup as anything other than a sexy girl, and type casting was a common complaint from most pinups trying to break into the industry. I know this was the case for me.

The first step in breaking into the industry is to acquire a good agent who will send you on auditions. However, the bigger and better the agent, the harder it is to obtain a meeting, much less get him or her to represent you. A good way to get agents to see you is through a good acting coach or a theatrical production. Getting a good acting coach can be expensive and time consuming, but if you are serious about film and television, there is no getting around that. Becoming a pinup opens a lot of doors for exposure, pardon the pun. Remember, opportunity meets preparation, and you must be more than a pretty girl to make it in such a competitive business.

In addition to acting classes, there is the expense of photos needed for an agent to sell you. A good theatrical and commercial headshot is a must. These pictures are not sexy, but rather wholesome and conservative—the kinds of photos that sell mainstream products not sex.

After photos and an acting coach are obtained, along with representation by a good agent or manager, you are ready to go on auditions, in hopes of booking a job. Keep in mind that television requires you to join the AFTRA union in order to perform television roles. Also, it is important to book something in a commercial or film with a speaking part in order to qualify for the all-important union SAG card.

Becoming a SAG member is a catch 22 and is essential to continue acting in mainstream movie roles. The easiest way to obtain the SAG card is through booking a television commercial. Most of the time, television commercials don't require speaking but rather a certain look and, therefore, can be somewhat easier to book. A good commercial agent is needed for these types of auditions.

Lots of actors do commercials because of the residual income. A commercial pays you every time it runs on television, so an actor may work one day on a commercial and receive residuals all year long from doing that one day's work. If you're lucky enough to book a frequently played commercial, you could buy a home with the ongoing residuals. A good national commercial can pay you for several weeks, months, or years, depending on the product, resulting in thousands of dollars for the actor.

Residual income is also very nice for television and movie roles that go straight to cable or DVD. However, it's difficult for actors to make a living just off of acting. Most actors have side jobs such as bartending, waiting tables, or modeling to make ends meet. A pinup has a jump start with the ability to model in a specific industry.

It is also important to take a look at the porn industry today and see how it has evolved. There is a fine line between what is porn and what is in the mainstream today. Porn stars such as Jenna Jameson and Tracy Lords made the jump from porn to mainstream television. The industry of porn today is a multi-billion-dollar industry and continues to grow. Movies are made for HBO and SHOWTIME that have explicit love scenes. Although they are simulated and the actors are not really having sex, these scenes can be just as explicit as an actual porn scene.

The pinup girl is not a porn star, although a few have become porn stars. The porn star really does have sex on camera, and a pinup model fakes it. A pinup is the softest of what some may consider porn. That is why Playboy's stamp of approval is necessary to hold a pinup in the highest regards. She is the elite of the elite, and how she chooses to be filmed can make her a legend. As a porn star, she could make fast money for a short time, but as a respected pinup, she could have residual income from her image for years to come.

I know some very famous and extremely successful and intelligent porn stars. This is a very diverse and interesting group of characters, that's for sure. I had the pleasure of meeting and playing cupid to porn star Asia Carrera. Asia was probably the shyest person I had ever met in my life! It was so hard for me to believe she was a porn star, until I saw her movies, of course. Asia had a genius IQ and was her own Web master, since she was a homebody computer geek. She had a social phobia and hardly ever spoke on the phone; but she would communicate warmly by e-mail.

My roommate, fitness expert Don Lemmon, and Asia had communicated online, and because they both had me in common, they decided to meet for lunch. I watched as a love affair developed pretty quickly, they married and named their second child Devin after me.. They recently informed me that they want to name this baby Devin because of my part in uniting them.

Getting to know Asia really educated me on what a porn star is. Asia didn't fit into the stereotypical character of a porn star. She was extremely intelligent, talented, and shy. Who knew? Some people get into porn to play against who they really are, and most of them will tell you that their sex life isn't the way it looks on camera. Some are extreme exhibitionists, and some just plainly love sex with many different people.

There are so many nude Web sites, and many mainstream actresses appear nude on screen. What was once taboo isn't so bad today. Playboy isn't the target of feminist groups and religious backlash as often today as it has been in the past decades.

Since the adult industry has grown into such a gigantic industry, some porn stars today can make millions, and many beautiful men and women are in porn. We must understand this industry in order to see the evolution of the pinup girl. She is in a league of her own. She is still an enigma and a fantasy to many.

The elite pinup girl would never do porn or have actual sex on camera. She must make sure not to tarnish her "girl next door" image. I have had simulated sex scenes on camera. My first sex scene was with actor Patrick Dempsey in *Can't Buy Me Love*. This high school comedy was done in 1987, and I was twenty-three years old. It was Patrick's first love scene as well, and he was nineteen. I remember talking about the scene beforehand, and we both were nervous, even though all we did was kiss.

The scene called for him to feel my breast, and I was topless on set. You would think that since I'd been in *Playboy* that this would have been a piece of cake for me. Well, it wasn't, and my shy side came out to torture me. I was a nervous wreck, but I learned a lot about doing a love scene in a film.

My second love scene in a film really taught me a lot more and expanded my insight to how difficult they could be. The film was called *Society*, starring soap star Billy Warlock. Billy had just won an Emmy award for the daytime soap *Days of Our Lives* and was a very good actor. This, however, was his first love scene in a film.

He was more nervous about doing it than I was, because soap actors usually have clothing on from the waist down. *Society* was also a high school comedy, but a dark comedy. Billy's character was losing his virginity to mine. The scene called for me to seduce him, and I was nude, with the exception of a tiny G-string.

There were about thirty crew people on the closed set, and the tension that was building with Billy was getting thick. This was not sexual tension; he was really self-conscious about doing this scene. I remember him saying that it was easy for me to do, which really offended me. I explained to him that this was my second love scene, and I too was extremely nervous about it. I tried to explain that just because a girl poses nude doesn't mean that doing an actual love scene in a film is easy. There is a big difference.

I think Billy was more self-conscious about acting out, having an orgasm in that scene, than anything else really. I, on the other hand, wanted to be professional and do the best job I could.

Society became a cult classic and got rave reviews all over the world. It was one of the strangest movies I've ever done, but I'm proud of the work I did in my first leading role.

Love scenes in movies can be tedious, and what you see on screen as sexy and sensual is due to editing. The scenes are often time consuming and totally non-sexual and non-sensual. I think most actors will tell you that doing them can be very hard sometimes. Having a room full of crew members watching me while I was trying to be sensuous in a love scene was difficult for me. I really don't like doing them, to tell you the truth.

As you can see, there is a big difference in doing porn and doing love scenes in a film. Just because a girl chooses to pose nude or becomes a pinup it doesn't make her a porn star.

I think the entertainment industry has changed a lot since my acting days in the mid '80s. More and more mainstream actors are doing sexy love scenes, and love scenes today are getting more and more explicit.

The most explicit love scene I ever did was for a movie called *The Passion Network*. Although it was a simulated sex scene, I kissed a woman in a threesome. I chose to do this film because I watched Jennifer Aniston kiss Winona Ryder on the TV show *Friends*. I saw that mainstream television was pushing the envelope. Since I had an adult Web site to feed, I thought this would be great for me to do as well. I was trying to reinvent myself and wanted to draw attention, so I decided to do this scene.

Today I'm pickier about what roles I play and feel there are way more opportunities for me than I had years ago. There are many Latin stars in film and television today, and no longer am I limited to being just the sexy pinup girl. I feel that I have gained a wealth of knowledge doing the love scenes I've done and am proud of my overall work as an actress.

I was the first woman to take my bra off on the hit TV series *Married with Children* in 1989. This caused a controversy, and a Michigan housewife wrote to sponsors, complaining that this new FOX show was distasteful. However, the controversy caused curious viewers to watch more of the show and kept it on the air for eleven years. I was told this was largely thanks to me. Looking back, it's easy to see how times have changed in television and film.

Cable television and pay-per-view have enabled viewers to pick and choose the programming that they want to pay for and watch. Shows such as *Sex and the City* and *Sopranos* changed the way we watch television as they displayed nudity and explicit language.

Still, mainstream network television remains more conservative because of sponsors. When Janet Jackson exposed her breast on a Super Bowl halftime show, CBS freaked out and all hell broke loose. This was just a breast and the nipple was covered, but the talk and jokes that surround this controversy are still brewing.

America's views on nudity in television, film, and advertising are still conservative in comparison to Europe. Europeans don't see the problem and often display nudity in their commercials, ads, and films. I know several mainstream actors and actresses who go to Europe and make a lot of money doing nudity in commercials and advertisements, especially if they have made a name for themselves here in America.

It's ironic that the pinup girl was born in America and is an American classic, but isn't taken seriously in film or television. There are exceptions, but on average it's hard for the pinup girl to break into mainstream film and television seriously.

She has to work harder than the average girl to prove herself, just because she's posed nude. That's why a pinup must carefully decide exactly what she wants in regards to film and television. Once the decision is made, she can take the necessary steps towards stardom, if that is her desire. It is plain to see that the pinup has many opportunities, and it's up to her to make good choices.

There are past pinups who showed potential as actresses but tragically died before their time, such as Dorothy Stratten and Claudia Jennings. Claudia was crowned "Playmate of the Year" in the early '70s and did a lot of B films. Claudia was praised by critics, and her career seemed very promising, but she died in a car crash. Dorothy was also crowned "Playmate of the Year" in 1980 and showed tremendous ability as an actress when cast opposite John Ritter in *They All Laughed*, which was directed by Peter Bogdonavich. An affair developed between Dorothy and the director, which led to her estranged husband's insane jealousy. Dorothy was brutally killed by her husband, who then killed himself. The movie *Star 80* depicted Dorothy's rise to fame and untimely death, and she became frozen in our minds as the perfect pinup. These women pioneered the way for pinups to star in film and television. Their promising careers and tragic deaths made them icons.

As the nineties rolled around, it was apparent that things were changing, and Hollywood changed with it. Pinups such as Pamela Anderson and Jenny McCarthy had their own television shows, endorsed mainstream products, and still posed nude. Playboy and Hugh Hefner became legendary pinup breeders, and the world wanted more sexy women to admire. It's easy to see why the pinup girl can be a star in film and television today, if she so desires.

I have witnessed lots of changes in Hollywood over the past twenty-five years. When I first started to act, you either did film or television. The crossover for an actress to do both was not as popular as it is today. It was very common for an actress to start out doing commercials and guest appearances on television. This gives an actress experience and credentials for her résumé. It was more prestigious to have film credits when I started my acting career; today it's very different. Many major stars not only do both television and film, but also produce and direct. The crossover into other areas of entertainment is quite common.

In the early days of Hollywood, many stars were groomed and taken care of by the major studios. The studios, such as Paramount and MGM, provided actors with classes and a weekly salary and placed them in roles to build their résumés. They made them stars. Today, an actor must be disciplined enough to do those things for himself or herself.

Today the pinup girl has more opportunities than ever; however, she must be disciplined enough to prepare for her big break if she wants to be a serious actress. The casting couch sometimes creates difficulties. The casting couch refers to being propositioned for sexual favors in return for a role. Many famous actresses have surrendered to the casting couch, but I personally never have. I refused to compromise my values for a role in film or television. It just wasn't ever going to happen.

I remember the first time I experienced the casting couch. I wasn't an actress; in fact, I had never had a role. I had just become a Playmate, and a very famous producer called Playboy, asking to meet me for a role. I was living in Chicago at the time, and I was flattered that this huge producer wanted to meet me. Playboy was very excited and urged me to come to Los Angeles immediately.

Prince and I were dating at the time, and he was kind enough to fly me out for this meeting. I remember being so nervous, since I had absolutely no acting experience and had never even seen a script!

I promptly arrived for my big meeting and waited in the producer's office, while he talked on the phone to a very famous director for forty-five minutes! This made me even more nervous, and I thought perhaps I'd be working with this big director. How cool would that be?

Finally, he got off of the phone to talk to me. He immediately asked about my relationship with Prince. I was so surprised that he knew about us. Prince was very private, and I didn't like to talk about him, but I did inform the producer that Prince had flown me to this meeting. He proceeded to be vague about this so-called role and showed me tickets to a movie premiere. I saw where this was going and politely made my exit.

It was obvious that he was more interested in trying to date me than casting me in a movie role. I was so pissed that I'd wasted that kind of time, but it taught me a valuable lesson. I was determined to make it on my own merit rather than sleep my way there. I figured the odds were really going to be against me, as far as acting went. It wasn't my passion in life, so I gave it up after only two years in Hollywood.

It is nice to see that things have changed and there are more opportunities. However, the casting couch will always be there to tempt you in some way, and you must be prepared for it.

Some people in power think they can have anything they want, and a lot of them want pinup girls. It's both a blessing and a curse sometimes; people make assumptions about you just because you've posed nude. Many pinups have dated high-profile producers, directors, or actors. This doesn't necessarily make you a star. Most of the time it's a drawback, and the girl is lucky to get anything directly from this.

I had a brief relationship with actor Sylvester Stallone and can attest to the fact that dating him didn't get me anywhere as an actress. In fact, dating a high-profile person can be rather difficult. You must deal with the press, tabloids, and girls who want to take your place constantly. I had to change my phone number several times when I dated Stallone; his ex-wife Bridget Nielson even called me! The experience proved too much for me to handle, and I got married and moved to Knoxville, Tennessee, shortly afterwards.

The glitter and glamour of Hollywood isn't what it appears sometimes. I wanted to have a simpler and more stable lifestyle. Looking back, I can see that I was overwhelmed by Hollywood and ran away out of fear. Many young girls who come to Hollywood looking for stardom may have felt the way I did. Many may not have been as lucky to prevail and sustain living and competing in such a fantasy world.

Reality television shows us what we may not have known about the real Hollywood. Shows that are devoted to a peek at a celebrity's life shed light on what was once fantasy.

I believe the computer will eventually merge with television, and very little will be left to the imagination. It is important to understand the media and know exactly what you want to do in it. Actors today are more in control of their image than ever before, so it's really up to the talent to decide how he or she wants to be viewed by the public. The average person has a chance at stardom today, since more and more people are involved in reality television.

Hit reality shows such as *Dancing with the Stars*, *American Idol*, and *America's Next Top Model* are really spinoffs of *Star Search*. America can vote for average people to be their next big star in modeling, singing, and dancing. This shows me how far television has come since my big win on *Star Search*.

The first time you saw an average person compete to be a professional in the entertainment business was on *Star Search*. Many *Star Search* contestants who didn't win the grand prize went on to become big stars, such as Britney Spears, Rosie O'Donnell, and Dennis Miller. Many got their big breaks on the show, such as Jenny Jones, Sinbad, and Tracey Ross. This was the first talent show on television that gave everyone a chance at stardom. *Star Search* stayed on the air for eleven years and was the grandfather of reality talent shows. My win on *Star Search* is one of my greatest achievements.

Playboy was so proud of me that I was presented on the cover in a celebrity feature. This was a big compliment to an ethnic Playmate at that time.

I believe my career could have been bigger had I stayed in Hollywood longer. Today, that kind of win could have boosted my career into more film and television, thanks to the Internet.

I remember people telling me that they were hoping I'd win when I was on the show. One of those people happened to be Paula Abdul. Paula was the choreographer on the film *Can't Buy Me Love*. She told me that she watched me on *Star Search* and was rooting for me to win. What a coincidence that Paula now gives the average person the chance to be a star on *American Idol*?

Today, online interaction from the viewers of a television show can make the winners of these reality talent shows megastars. Old television stars can have another crack at stardom through reality television. Reality television now has its own award shows, so I believe it's here to stay.

I have known some reality stars who have given up their jobs to pursue acting. Seems everyone wants their fifteen minutes of fame, and with the extension of cable television, reality television, and the Internet, that is now possible.

The most important thing to understand when breaking into film or television is that it is a business. It may seem glamorous and exciting to many, but it is a tough business to be in. Most people cannot make a living from it, and the competition is greater now than ever. So it is important to have a game plan when entering show business, and know and understand the business aspect of it. Knowledge is power, and if a girl can learn enough about the business and understand how to work it, she can be successful.

Your image is a commodity in and of itself because you are selling you. Always keep that in mind, and learn as much as you can about the business part of entertainment. You must strive to always be better tomorrow than you are today.

Website photo

Theatrical headshot

Commercial headshot

Body shot

My favorite headshot

Chapter Eight: Branding An Icon

I hope you can now see and understand what is reality and what is fantasy about a pinup. No one else has the opportunities a pinup girl has, and a select few can become legends in the future if they understand certain things about the business. One of those things is branding. A celebrity can now brand his or her image to be instantly recognized. Branding is carving a unique image into our minds like Playboy, Levi's, or Revlon—a certain image comes to mind when we think of these brands.

A few years ago, I had the privilege of interviewing legend Bettie Page, but I had to first be interviewed by her agent, Mark Roesler. Mark and I quickly became good friends, and I learned a lot about branding an image from him. Mark is the CEO of CMG Worldwide, a company devoted to licensing and merchandising living and dead celebrities. They have offices in Indianapolis, Hollywood, and Rio. Some of their clients include Marilyn Monroe, James Dean, Babe Ruth, and Sophia Loren.

Mark is an attorney who was once a roofer! Mark saw how the public couldn't get enough of Elvis Presley's merchandise after his death and understood that this was big business. He realized that there was no one representing dead celebrities and rallied to change laws that protected a celebrity's image and the use of that image after death. Elvis died in debt, but because of the laws that protect the images of dead celebrities, the Elvis Presley estate is now worth hundreds of millions of dollars, and that control is in the hands of his family.

Since he was from Indiana and a big James Dean fan, he started with James Dean. Seems James Dean died while still under contract with Warner Brothers, so there was a question about who really owned his image; was it the studio or his family? Mark had to tackle Warner Brothers for the rights to James Dean's images, in order to hand them over to Dean's family. Because of that victory, the families of all living and dead celebrities are now protected.

Mark Roesler is a respected expert in the field of licensing and merchandising a celebrity. Because of this, he has been called to testify as an expert witness in many high-profile celebrity trials, such as the OJ Simpson civil suit. Such cases have made Mark a leading authority in protecting a celebrity's image and determining the value of his or her brand.

Mark explained to me that a celebrity has the "rights of publicity," which is an intangible and valuable asset to a celebrity. "Rights of publicity" is a law used to protect a celebrity from the unauthorized use of his or her name and likeness for commercial gain. In other words, someone can't put my picture on a pair of jeans for profit without my consent. It protects a famous person from being exploited by anyone for profit and puts the celebrity in control of his or her image.

The value of a celebrity's image will vary over time, depending on how successful that celebrity is and will be in the future. For example, Marilyn Monroe's image, as we all know, is all over the place on a variety of collectible merchandise. It is up to the Marilyn Monroe estate to approve such merchandise and, therefore, benefit from the licensing ventures created from her images, even after her death. Marilyn is an instant and recognized brand, and profits from sales have proven to be tremendous and have grown over time.

Mark Roesler's efforts to protect the rights of a celebrity's image have made him a pioneer in this field. Hugh Hefner and Anna Nicole Smith are both clients of CMG Worldwide, and Mark represents them.

A celebrity can make millions from endorsement deals. These deals link a celebrity's image with a product, usually in advertisements or commercials—for example, Anna Nicole Smith's endorsement deal

The Naked Truth About A Pinup Model

with the diet company Trim Spa. America watched her ballooned weight drop dramatically on her reality show, and she said she owed it all to Trim Spa. Billboards, commercials, and print ads for the diet company plastered the new and trim Anna Nicole all over the place, and she got paid very well for it. It's very common for celebrities to endorse products, and depending on the celebrity, the price tag can be enormous.

All of these things go hand in hand with branding a celebrity's image. Marilyn Monroe's value is worth more now than when she was alive. Her name, likeness, and unique persona have made her a worldwide icon of great value. Marilyn is Mark Roesler's biggest client, and it's easy to see why. We can learn from the past and see how to market and sell a celebrity's image today.

Mark also explained to me that copyrights were important to understand, especially by a pinup such as myself. When you are a celebrity, the paparazzi and fans will take photos of you constantly, but who owns those photos? The person taking the picture owns the photo, and thus the "copyright." The photos taken of celebrities by the paparazzi can be considered public domain, which means they are published photos. Copyrights can also involve art, music, or sculptures. It is important to understand the ownership of copyrights, especially involving photography. Since a pinup's image is photographed numerous times, the copyrights of ownership can be valuable to her brand in the future. Most pinups now have Web sites, and a Web site needs photo images. No longer is *Playboy* the only source of photography in regards to a pinup. She can now control her own image and own the copyrights of those images.

I use a variety of photographers for my own Web site. Some images I pay for and therefore own the rights to, and others I share the rights with the photographer. In other words, I use the photos for my own merchandise, and they can use the photos for their own merchandise. I pay a flat fee to some photographers for their services, and I own the rights completely. This is in essence what Playboy has done for years. They pay staff photographers a salary for their services, and Playboy owns all copyrights of their photos. They can use and reuse the photos as they wish. They can create Playboy merchandise with various photos of Playmates, because they own the copyrights.

Mark showed me an example of copyrights in regards to a celebrity's image, using Marilyn Monroe. He licensed the famous Marilyn Monroe *Playboy* centerfold on a bottle of wine, called "Marilyn Merlot." Since that photo was bought by Playboy to use in its first issue, they did not own the copyright; the photographer did. Mark had to get permission from the photographer, not Playboy, for the rights to that particular merchandising product.

Another example was that of a pair of pants with Marilyn's image on them. Seems a clothing brand, Nicole Miller, bought fabric from Italy with Marilyn's image and made these cool pants, without the Marilyn Monroe estate's approval. The company was sued by Marilyn's estate and the pants were taken off the market. It was actually an innocent mistake, since Nicole Miller didn't realize that the fabric they purchased with Marilyn's images were not legally approved by her estate and therefore couldn't be used for commercial profit.

Mark explained that this is all part of "intellectual property rights" of a celebrity. Branding an image involves understanding the rights of publicity, copyrights, and trademarks of a celebrity's image. It is a celebrity's right to control his or her image and the intangible value of that image, while living or dead.

The ownership of a celebrity's image, or copyright, is also important to understand because of merchandising. Certain Marilyn Monroe images can be used on a variety of merchandise, depending on who owns the image. Never-before-seen photos are always of value to Mark and the Marilyn Monroe estate, and deals are worked out with the photographers for the use of those images.

I have become friends with a former Playmate from the '60s named Susan Bernard. Susan is the sole heir and daughter of famous photographer Bernard of Hollywood. He photographed some of the most famous Hollywood starlets, including Marilyn Monroe. His images are used in a variety of merchandise, and there is a business relationship between Mark and Susan for some of Bernard's images of Marilyn.

Sometimes if the photographer is unknown or deceased, an image of a famous person will then be public domain, and therefore anyone can use it without copyright infringement. But if the photographer is alive or someone controls his estate, then his photos are protected by copyright and must be negotiated for commercial use.

As you can see, it is important to understand what these things mean in regards to protecting your image and producing merchandise. The images a celebrity owns and controls are of more value in the long run. The bigger his or her name becomes, the more merchandising possibilities arise.

History has proven with Marilyn Monroe that the potential profits of such a celebrity can be worth a bundle in the future. I personally believe that the future will prove to be profitable for more pinups who are smart about controlling their brand, such as Pamela Anderson.

The possibilities are endless, because of technology and the thirst for collecting memorabilia. The evening gowns, lingerie, shoes, and other personal items of a celebrity can sell for big bucks. Many high-profile stars now endorse clothing, whereas models once did. The crossovers for actors to models and models to actors are very commonplace today.

It seems the more recognized and valuable a celebrity's name is, the more money there is to be made from his or her image. So now that pinups are in the mainstream, the possibilities for them to make money in the future are endless.

I have watched Mark market Bettie Page through her Web site with a variety of merchandise such as T-shirts, handbags, lunch boxes, dolls, calendars, greeting cards, and hundreds of other items. The demand grows daily. Mark has been smart about branding her image on the same type of product as Marilyn's, which has already proven to be profitable.

Trading card

Playboy trading card

Calendar shot

Playboy Cover

Mark Roesler

Chapter Nine: The Future of Pinup

It's clear to see that pinup is here to stay. The past fifty years have shown us how powerful the pinup girl is, so it's safe to say she will be even more so in the future. Marilyn Monroe is and always will be the pioneer of it all, along with Playboy. It's no wonder that Hugh Hefner wants to be laid to rest right next to Marilyn, a final resting place in history. The gravesite is in Westwood, California, and Dorothy Stratten is also laid there. I visited the site once and felt a mysterious and strange feeling.

I too am a part of this history. The history of the fantasy girl and all that she is and ever will be is a part of me. I've watched it change and evolve over the past twenty-five years, and it's become bigger than I could ever have imagined. Since they say "history repeats itself," I can only foresee a long and bright future for the precious few who will prevail.

I think as a society, we are embracing our human sexuality. We are becoming more honest about who we really are as a species. A beautiful sexy female will always get attention, especially from the male gender. We as women must embrace our power, and that power has a lot to do with the naked eye. The wonderment of a pinup girl lies in how she captures us, how self-assured she is about her own nakedness, and how truly powerful that is.

Many people are drawn to that kind of raw honesty. It's time that America grows up and sees how dogmatic and ignorant it is to not view the female body as anything but beautiful. Europeans understand the female form and have appreciated the nude female in many beautiful works of art. They have nude beaches and nude females all over the place in advertisements. They understand that sex is a natural part of the human race.

America is still a young country, and its naive conservative views have to be revised. We must get with the program and see how much we've grown and how we're still growing. It's pretty obvious what is selling in media. We can't seem to get enough of sexy celebrities.

Reality television is making just about anything entertainment. Sexy and sensual women are more popular than ever, with hit shows such as *Sex and the City* and *Desperate Housewives*. Women are more empowered in the twenty-first century because of how much we all have grown.

The pinup is still in a special league all her own. She also shows us how much America has grown in its views, since we can now view nudity, especially the female form, as a positive part of humanity. We are all human and realize sex and nudity are natural. We want to see and experience this. The success of cable television shows us that most Americans will happily pay a monthly fee to view sex and nudity. No longer is it taboo to see nudity on television.

There are so many men's magazines today; *Playboy* no longer controls that market. The success, however, has made Hugh Hefner a living legend, and we are watching his every move at age eighty! It is amazing to see Hef living and recreating his lifestyle with his three girlfriends. He invented his own fantasy and actually got to live it! How many people actually achieve that in a lifetime?

I think that is why so many men admire Hef and Playboy. He and his empire represent an innocent era when we all discovered the "sexual revolution." The women who pioneered the way, like Marilyn and Bettie, are heroes to all women today, representing a braveness that most women couldn't even think of at the time.

Today, women are free to be who they are. It doesn't matter what their background is, their race, social status, or public opinion; a woman is free to do as she chooses. Nude modeling is viewed as artistic today, as it was in the days of Michelangelo and Van Gogh.

The pinup girl is confident about her body and uses it to make art, not pornography. She embodies a mystery of sensual allure that draws you into her world. She is admired by all for her presence is powerful and stands on its own. Men adore her, and women want to be her. She shows us that fantasy can be a reality if we so desire. She defines what is sexy, beautiful, artistic, fashionable, and erotic. She inspires men to achieve greatness and women to be great. She is a goddess among all for all to admire.

I'm sure if Marilyn were alive today, we would still be fascinated. As time moves forward, we will see other notable pinups from the '60s to the present pass on and leave behind their legacy. The unique lives they led and their influence on society won't be evident until later. It is safe to say the pinup model will conquer more in the future and achieve greater heights.

Women are powerful beings, and when we understand just how powerful we are, nothing is impossible to achieve. No longer is it a man's world; a woman has the freedom to be anything she so desires in the twenty-first century. She is in control of her destiny, and she can be as sexy as she wants to be.

The pinup girl represents freedom, and so it's fitting that she was inspired by men at war who put her photos in their lockers. Those soldiers fighting for America's freedom wanted to get back home to their dream girl. The pinup gave them that inspiration to keep fighting and to keep dreaming, because dreams do come true. My friendship with the Navy Lt. has given me more insight about our soldiers. He told me that it is what keeps them going and inspires them to keep fighting for our great country.

The rabbit head is a symbol that is recognized worldwide and is very much a part of our American culture. Hugh Hefner is admired by the young and old today. He is a living example of the American dream and what is possible. Many Playboy Playmates and bunnies have gone on to have successful careers thanks to Playboy. Hefner gave women the opportunity to be free at a time when there was very little freedom available for them. The diehard feminists attacked the magazine and

Hugh Hefner for years because of it, but more than a half of a century has proven that freedom prevails.

Playboy and the rabbit head will forever be symbols of what is America. The Playboy Playmate will forever define what a pinup is supposed to be, and she will keep that fantasy alive for years to come. Her legacy as part of the American dream and what makes America so unique is apparent. She will continue to influence, define, and capture those who bare witness to her baring it all. Legends and icons will evolve throughout the future and clearly help us understand how important the pinup girl has been and forever will be to our culture.

I am grateful to have been a part of this American dream. I understand how the pinup has grown and can clearly see my own future as bright and beautiful with the freedom to become the best I can possibly be and not be ashamed of my naked honesty. I feel proud to be an American woman, to be such a major part of the American sexual revolution, and to be a pinup for future pinups to admire. Who knows what the future holds for me, but one thing is certain: I do know that dreams do come true. They did for me and can for you.

Chapter Eleven:
Anna Nicole Smith

I felt it was necessary to include a chapter on the late Anna Nicole Smith, who died mysteriously in a hotel room on February 8, 2007, in Hollywood, Florida.

Anna seemed to have an affinity with the great Marilyn Monroe. Early in her career, she was often compared to Marilyn and seemed destined to have tragedy in life like Marilyn. Anna depicts, like Marilyn, the irony of life imitating art in her likeness and what others will remember of her image. Unlike Marilyn, Anna had a very hard time with the law. Her later life was mostly filled with courtroom dramas, lawyers, and battles that took her all the way to the Supreme Court.

Anna's bigger-than-life persona took over and overshadowed anything she did as a model or an actress. Her tabloid life and her ballooning weight took the focus. However, it's important to note that Anna was indeed a unique pinup for the end of the twentieth century.

I met Anna only once, at her "Playmate of the Year" luncheon. She was at the peak of her career as the Guess jeans model and there were over seventy Playmates attending her luncheon, the biggest number ever! I guess most of the other girls were as curious as I was to see her in person. I remember thinking how different she looked from everyone else, so full-figured and such a flashback of that '50s era. It was apparent to see why she was such a rage; she was absolutely beautiful!

She reminded everyone of Marilyn and even had on a white dress similar to Marilyn's famous one in *The Seven Year Itch*. Anna was as big as Texas, which is where she was from. I felt like one of her boobs was as big as my whole chest. She was a tall girl, and everything about her was big! Her face was big and beautiful, and her body was also. She was unlike girls of today, and there was no doubt she was going to be a star.

It wasn't long before movie roles surfaced, such as her black-and-white appearance in *The Hudsucker Proxy*, which seemed promising. We all wanted her to succeed and rooted for her.

But, it wasn't long before she was all over the tabloids when she married, at twenty-five, a billionaire oil tycoon who was in his nineties. Her husband died shortly after the wedding, and the press had a field day covering the nasty court battle between Anna and her stepson for her husband's inheritance.

Anna was dubbed the richest Playmate when she stood to inherit over a half-billion dollars. The press followed her every move, and the court battle became her cross to bear for the rest of her life. Her weight ballooned to over 300 pounds, and frivolous lawsuits against her followed. She became a tabloid joke, and then came *The Anna Nicole Show*.

The Anna Nicole Show was the first reality show on E Entertainment with high ratings. It depicted Anna, her son Daniel, lawyer Howard K. Stern, assistant Kim, and her dog Sugar Pie as her family. She let the world see for themselves who she really was and what her life was like. Her IQ didn't seem too high, and her taste was big, gaudy, and sometimes vulgar. Her life seemed sad and destined to be tragic, yet we couldn't stop watching and waiting for it to unfold.

Then Anna's show was cancelled and she was again in the news with her court battles. She surprised everyone by dropping nearly seventy pounds from her TrimSpa diet. She looked so good that TrimSpa made her their spokesmodel, and her career seemed to be on the rise again with billboards, commercials, and appearances. However, it was hard to not notice a distinctive slur in her speech, which made you wonder if drugs were involved.

She continued her quest to win her inheritance, and since her stepson was now deceased, her fight seemed promising, especially when the Supreme Court ruled that she should get another day in court. Anna Nicole never got that day in court, but her case and her death have changed the way law school students study. They are now studying Anna Nicole and her battles in court, which ironically remain even after her death.

Since she and her son Daniel died so mysteriously within five months of each other, the death of Anna Nicole Smith remains a much-talked-about subject. Howard K. Stern, her lawyer, constant companion, and supposed father of her daughter, born just before her son Daniel died, is now the focus of the media and courtroom as he battles the paternity of the child against Anna's former boyfriend Larry Birkhead.

This ongoing reality courtroom drama still has everyone talking about Anna Nicole Smith. Her estranged mother even jumped in on the courtroom battle for the burial site of Anna's body, and several other men claimed to be the father of her baby girl, Dannielynn. A very sad ending to a life that seemed so promising. In the end, Larry Birkhead proved to be the child's father.

Anna had the world watching her every move in life and now in death. Like her idol, Marilyn Monroe, she died tragically at age thirty-nine and will be remembered for her outrageous life battles more than anything. She was, however, a pinup model and one who will be remembered and cherished fondly by fans forever. Like Bettie Page and Marilyn, her images are ingrained in our minds and won't be forgotten. Mark Roeseler also represented Anna Nicole, and like Bettie and Marilyn, Anna will live on in photos, merchandise, and art portraying her images that we fell in love with.

Anna is my Playmate sister, and for all the fans who loved her, may she finally rest in peace.

Anna Nicole Smith

Anna Nicole Smith

Chapter Ten:
A Conversation With Bettie

I first met Bettie Page in March of 2002 at the CMG Worldwide offices in Los Angeles. Bettie and I had a few conversations on a three-way call with her agent, Mark Roesler. She was seventy-eight years old and her health was failing. Mark explained that she didn't get out much at all, so it was quite an honor to be granted this interview.

I intended to make a documentary on the evolution of the pinup girl, from a pinup girl's point of view. I figured half of my own life was spent being a pinup model, and I saw that this had never been done before. Bettie was quite impressed that someone like myself had chosen to interview her; this was the first and only time someone who had done what she did was interviewing her. She seemed excited about it.

I remember waiting anxiously for Bettie to get to the offices; she was over an hour late, and Mark explained that he had to go and pick her up, and whether or not she showed up depended on her mood. I guess it was my lucky day.

I recognized that face immediately, even though the famous bangs were totally gray. Her bright blue eyes and the red lipstick she was wearing left no doubt that she was the one and only Bettie Page. Though she was seventy-eight, her face looked fifty.

Her thick southern accent brought out my own Louisiana drawl. I found her to be very talkative and lucid. She could remember dates and went into great detail when answering my questions. She loved talking about that time in her life, and we had a great afternoon chatting. She seemed impressed to hear about Dita Von Teese and other pinups who are today emulating her style.

Throughout the years following, I had the honor of going out to dinner with Bettie and Mark Roesler. She loved to talk about dieting and was very smart about nutrition. She ate only organic foods and read a lot of spiritual and nutritional books.

She still had a zest for life and loved to "smell the roses" as she put it. She told me how much she loved to dance, and it was only because of the natural aging process that she wasn't as active as she would have liked to have been.

Bettie's life reads like a movie script. She lived quite an interesting life, and most people only knew a fraction of who she really was. I chose to talk about the positive part of Bettie's life and why we love her. Like Marilyn, there was tragedy in Bettie's life. She didn't like to talk about those years, and I didn't want her to. Unlike Marilyn, Bettie lived to be an old lady who had lived a very full life. We can only learn from it.

Following is a little of what we talked about during that first interview.

Devin: You are an icon in the pinup world, Bettie. How do you feel about that?

Bettie: I don't know why they call me a legend or an icon; I don't even know what an icon is. I'm amazed that I was singled out. It's never happened to any other model. I made more money in the recent years than I did during the seven years I modeled in New York. It amazes me that I am now represented by CMG Worldwide, who handles the most famous people in the world like Marilyn Monroe! Mark Roesler is always bringing me books, art pieces, and a variety of other items with my photos on them. It's hard for me to autograph a lot of things due to my arthritis, but I do manage to do some things. I get such a kick out of how famous I am today. Who would have thought this would happen?

Devin: Why did you disappear, Bettie?

Bettie: I never disappeared! It was two weeks before Christmas in 1957. I thought there were too many pictures of me. I thought the photographers were getting tired of photographing me and decided I needed a change. I was thirty-four, and I decided to visit my sister in Florida and give my life to Jesus. I went to Bible school and dedicated my life to the Lord. There were many fantastic stories about what happened to me, such as I was living in a trailer park in Kentucky, that I was part of a harem in India, or married to Irving Klaw. That story went around for years, believe it or not. I just simply wanted a different life.

Devin: Did you know that you have influenced fashion because of your famous bangs?

Bettie: It's funny how my famous bangs came about. I was modeling for Jerry Tibbs, the black police officer from Brooklyn who discovered me on the beach. He told me I had a very high forehead and would look better if I had bangs. I went home and cut me some bangs and have been wearing them ever since!

Devin: What do you think of the fashion and pinup models that try to imitate you?

Bettie: I'm flattered that they would. It makes me feel good, of course. I find it funny that Madonna was wearing those cones in her bra on stage; they were replicas of the costumes I used to make for my shoots back in the fifties. I love to look at the fashion models that have been inspired by me, and I hear there is a pinup model named Dita who is the new Bettie Page today. It's funny to see some of the leather costumes that the fashion models wear on the runway today, 'cause they were exactly like the ones I used to pose in for Irving Klaw.

Devin: How would you like to be remembered, Bettie?

Bettie: I would most like to be remembered as someone who created my own poses. Now some people, like Bunny Yeager and others, have said that they taught me how to pose. No one taught me how to pose; everything I did was what I created from imitating famous movie stars and making up my own style of posing. My sisters and I used to play 'program' and we would imitate the movie stars we saw in the National Tennessee newspaper. I didn't want to do the same old poses, so I was always trying to create something new and different, especially if a photographer uses me a lot.

Devin: Why are you so reclusive today?

Bettie: I would like people to remember how I was in the photos, not as I am today. I'm old and gray and need to lose some weight, plus I have so many doctors to see for all my aging problems that it's difficult for me to get out and smell the roses. I would love nothing more than to smell the roses, but it's simply not possible at times. I do sometimes make it up to the Playboy Mansion; that's always fun for me.

Devin: What do you think of the Internet and nudity today?

Bettie: I think the Internet should be regulated and that there is too much promiscuity in photos today; seems anything goes! In the fifties, it was a sin or worse for a girl to pose nude, and the pubic hair was never shown. I was called a slut, sinner, and everything else for posing nude. I didn't look at it that way. I thought, when God created Adam and Eve, they were nude. I bet when he walked with them in the Garden of Eden that he was nude too! I always had fun doing the photos. However, I don't like the promiscuity in photos today. We didn't even think of doing open poses with the legs spread open back then. I think it should go back to how it was in the fifties. I don't like seeing all the implants in the breasts and how top heavy most pinup models are today.

Devin: What do you think of today's pinup models?

Bettie: I think men like a woman to have natural breasts; we didn't even know what an implant was in the fifties. A small waist and not so skinny is what the pinup girls looked like in my day. I got my figure from working out with weights and swimming. I loved to dance and play sports, and I could eat whatever I wanted to back then. Today most of the girls have those implants in the breasts and are too top heavy and too skinny.

Devin: What do you think of Playboy and Hugh Hefner?

Bettie: I think it's amazing what he created for himself with Playboy, and I'm happy to be a part of it. He sure knows how to throw a party. It's amazing how he finds all those beautiful girls to pose for the magazine. In my day, it was unusual for a woman to pose nude at all, and the pubic hair was always covered in photos.

Devin: You came to Hollywood and wanted to be an actress. Do you have any juicy stories to tell?

Bettie: Well, I was propositioned by Howard Hughes. I turned him down and thought he was weird. Maybe I would have made it as an actress if I had, but I believed in love. People thought I must have been wild and had a lot of sex because of my posing nude. I had only a few men in my entire life. It's funny, they call me the innovator of sex and photos. I had less sex in the seven years I modeled than I did in my whole life. I was dating one man pretty much the entire time.

Devin: How do you feel being interviewed by someone like myself who has posed nude also?

Bettie: I think it's fantastic, unique, and very original for someone as famous as you to want to do a book and documentary on the pinup girl. I've only been interviewed by photographers and news media people. You are the first woman who has done what I have done in modeling to interview me, and you should be proud of that.

Devin: What do you think the pinup girl represents today?

Bettie: I think the pinup model represents a free and powerful woman today, more so than she was in my day. There are so many models posing nude today. There are even actresses and fashion models who pose nude today. That wasn't the case in my era. I believe the true pinup model should never do open poses or appear in pornography type of photographs. She must always have class in her photos. The human body is nothing to be ashamed of, and with all the artists such as Olivia who have painted me, I feel flattered. I was very proud of my figure and worked hard to keep it in shape. Today, there is so much plastic surgery that it's hard to tell what's real and what's not. But I think the true essence of a woman is to be a woman with curves in the right places. That is what the pinup girl is all about.

Devin: Bettie, will you sign my Playmate book? You will be the first Playmate to do so for me.

Bettie: Sure, what would you like me to say?

Devin: Say, "To my adopted daughter, love Bettie Page."

Bettie: (laughs) Since I never had children, I think I can do that!

My relationship with Bettie lasted almost seven years. Occasionally, we would go out to dinner with her agent, Mark Roesler, and dine at the Sizzler. Sometimes I would send over chili or chicken soup for her because she loved my cooking. Bettie had simple tastes and used to say, "You need to stop and smell the roses in life, Devin." She enjoyed going to the Playboy Mansion for the parties and loved telling us stories about her modeling days. I think it's because she was the happiest when she was modeling and knew she was good at it.

Although her health was failing, she was determined to be healthy. She loved to shop at organic supermarkets, had a passion for reading nutrition books, and took lots of vitamins. She would say, "I want to live to be a healthy one hundred years old." But, due to her ongoing health problems, it was a rare occasion that Bettie would feel good enough to leave her small apartment.

Mark and I would visit her sometimes and bring the latest new and exciting Bettie Page product to her that was on the fast-growing Bettie-mania market. She would sign photos and artwork for Mark.

The Naked Truth About A Pinup Model

She would get such a kick out of how popular she still was and was always in awe of it. But those visits were seldom and became few and far between in the last couple of years before her death.

Mark and I would run into each other at the Playboy parties, and he would always fill me in on how she was doing. The last time I saw her at the Playboy Mansion was for a private screening of the HBO film *The Notorious Bettie Page*. There were only a select few people there who were invited, so I felt honored. I was with my boyfriend Ronn Moss, and we were sitting near Bettie, who talked throughout the whole film. She would blurt out things like, "Is that supposed to be me? She doesn't look anything like me." She started to get upset as the movie progressed and said, "How did they know that? I only told one person." Or, "That's a lie!" She began to speak louder and louder and got increasingly upset, so much so that Mark had to abruptly escort her out of the mansion because she didn't want to see any more of it.

Mark was sweating bullets as he turned to me and asked me to help him. I had a way of calming her down, I guess. So I put my hand on her shoulder and said, "It's okay, Bettie. It's just a movie." But she was so upset she was crying and wanted to get out of there. That was the last time I saw her at the Playboy Mansion.

After numerous reports on her declining health from Mark, I knew I'd probably not see her again in the state of mind that she was once in. I knew I was lucky to have had those precious moments with such an amazing lady who brought so much to our American culture.

On Easter of 2008, I was told that Bettie was back in the mental hospital and wasn't able to care for herself anymore. Her health was now rapidly declining and she hadn't long to live. However, Bettie was a fighter, and somehow she managed to survive a stroke that paralyzed her from the neck down. She was moved to a hospital in Santa Monica, and Mark told me I could go and visit her.

Although I lived an hour and half away from Santa Monica, I felt that I should go as soon as possible, for the look on Mark's face told me I didn't have time to waste. Ronn and I went to visit her the very next day. Mark tried to prepare me for the visit and told me that she couldn't speak very well, would cry a lot, and of course couldn't move from the paralysis. However, nothing could have prepared me for that first visit.

She clearly had deteriorated to just a glimpse of who she was. Her mouth was slightly open all the time from the paralysis, but those baby blue eyes were still there. Ronn and I talked to her and read the Bible to her. She started to cry. We brought her roses from our rose garden. She didn't say anything, and I wasn't sure if she really knew who I was.

The soap opera *The Young and The Restless* was playing on the television screen. I pointed to Ronn and said, "Bettie, do you remember Ronn? He's on *The Bold and The Beautiful*." I told her his show came on after the one that was on the TV and pointed to the television. It seemed like she understood and followed intently with her eyes, but we still were not sure. That visit lasted about twenty minutes, and I asked the nurse to make sure Ronn's show would be on every day for her to watch.

We then met Mark and his wife, Stacey, for lunch to discuss the visit. Personally I felt she had no quality of life left and didn't want her to linger too long in that state. Sadly, I wanted her to pass quickly and expressed this to Mark, who said she had pneumonia and didn't have long to live. The way it looked at that time, we thought she had days left.

I e-mailed the artist Olivia and her husband, Joel, and informed them that Bettie was gravely ill and that if they wanted to see her one last time, they should do it immediately. It was a couple days before Halloween, and I had a bad dream about Bettie. Ronn said I cried out in my sleep, so loudly that I woke him up. I think seeing Bettie in the state she was in really took its toll on my emotions, and I worried that she would die alone. I didn't want that for her. I didn't want her to be alone. I guess I felt a kindred connection to her because we had so much in common. I too had never borne children, was sexually abused by my step father, and was in foster homes. My own mother has a history of mental illness; and I too loved my pinup modeling days.

I told Ronn and Mark that I wanted to visit her again and read the Bible to her. I wanted to encourage her to not be afraid of death and to know she was not alone. Mark agreed to give me access to visit her anytime we wished and informed us that she had been moved to another hospital in Santa Monica due to a high fever and breathing problems.

Ronn and I rushed to see her at the new hospital and got stuck in traffic. When we finally got there, we were told she was taken to yet another hospital in Culver City where she would get the special care she needed. We finally arrived at the Kindred hospital; I thought the name was appropriate to how I was feeling.

We were surprised to see that Bettie was sharing a room with another elderly patient. She was alert, but felt feverish. Ronn got a washcloth and wet it with cold water to wash her face. She seemed to like that and made cooing sounds. I read the Bible to her, and we both just kept telling her how much she was loved and that she was not alone. We could tell after about a half hour that she was getting sleepy, so we said our goodbyes.

I thought that would be the last time we would see her. Then Mark called me and asked if I would speak with a documentary filmmaker, Mark Mori from New York, who was doing a film on Bettie. Mori and I spoke on the phone, and he came over to meet me at my home. He showed us footage he had been collecting on Bettie and an interview he had done years prior. We told him of our last visit with her, and he expressed an interest in going to visit her before he caught his flight back to New York.

So we decided to take him for a visit. Mark Roesler met us there. This visit was uniquely different in that Bettie actually tried to speak. She seemed like she was much better than during our last visit. It was mid November now, and I was simply amazed that she was still hanging on in this condition. The doctors were also amazed and said a high fever and pneumonia at her age would do most people in, but Bettie was still fighting and defying the odds.

After that visit, Ronn and I decided to visit her every week, and it was pretty much the same ritual. Depending on how alert she was, she would respond to us with a few words and with her eyes. Ronn would wash her face, and I would read the Bible.

On November 22, 2008, Ronn and I were going to a black-tie wedding in Santa Monica and thought we would stop and see Bettie. I was in an evening gown, and Ronn was in a tux. We walked into the room, and Bettie's eyes lit up. She seemed happy to see us. I said, "Bettie, doesn't Ronn look handsome in a tux?" She replied, "He looks good in anything." We were so surprised to hear her put a sentence together. She looked at me and said, "You look beautiful." I was so thrilled to see her trying to talk to us. We showed her photos on my phone of my little dog, Romeo. She said, "Oh, he looks so cute!" We told her we had horses, and she said, "I love horses." There was no doubt she understood us and was communicating with us that day. It was like her mind and spirit were trapped in this wretched body that didn't serve her any longer. But our Bettie was still there with us.

We had our longest visit with Bettie that day, almost an hour. Then suddenly the machines were beeping, and the elderly lady next to us was begging for ice and asking for help. Ronn went to find a nurse, and finally the elderly lady calmed down. Then she asked me if I was Bettie's daughter. We chatted for a while, and she thanked us for helping her. I felt happy that we had such a wonderful visit with Bettie and grateful that I had those precious moments with her and Ronn.

A couple of days later, Mark told me that she went into cardiac arrest and was revived, but that she was now brain dead. He said if I wanted to see her one last time I should do it immediately because she was now in the ICU on life support.

Ronn and I immediately went to the ICU to visit Bettie for what we knew would be our final visit. We had seen her several times now, and the thought of her finally leaving us was apparent and welcomed. But, seeing her on the life support with covering over her eyes made us both feel that she was no longer here in spirit like she was only a few days before. I knew that was her way of saying goodbye to us. I read the Twenty-third Psalm of the Bible to her, and just as we were leaving, her friend Carlo came in to also say goodbye.

He seemed a bit shocked to see her because he had not seen her since they were neighbors, and it was clear he didn't expect her to be as bad as she was. He read a poem that he said was one of her favorites, and we all said our final goodbye to Bettie.

On the way home, I felt relieved to know that she would soon be out of that body. I also told Ronn of my own fears that I had of growing old and being helpless after seeing Bettie so many times.

Mark said he was in Florida and was on his way back to Bettie; they would be taking her off of life support. However, it took a couple of days longer than expected before they actually took her off due to the fact that some of her family wasn't here. Bettie had a brother in Tennessee and a sister in Georgia, as well as a niece.

I offered my help to Mark with funeral arrangements. He discussed what kind of pictures he should use on the program and got Doctor Schuller, whom Bettie loved, to do the service. She was a devout Christian, and we had gone to see "The Glory of Christmas" and "The Glory of Easter" for which Doctor Schuller gave sermons. Mark wanted Ronn to do some music for the service and also had the guy who did some music with bagpipes in the movie *Braveheart* to play "Amazing Grace" as well as a couple of other songs. We both thought cremation was best, but Mark also wanted a coffin. The service would be small, and invited guests included Hugh Hefner, Olivia, and close friends and relatives. The service would be held in the chapel at the Pierce Brothers mortuary in Westwood—the same location as the services for Marilyn Monroe, Dorothy Stratten, Natalie Wood, and Jack Lemmon, to name a few. It would also be the final resting place for Hugh Hefner, who bought the crypt next to Marilyn Monroe several years ago. So we thought it was fitting to have Bettie there also.

Bettie was taken off of life support on December 11, 2008, and the doctors thought it would take minutes for her to expire. However, several hours later, Bettie was still alive! It took nearly ten hours before she finally passed away, still defying the odds and surprising the doctors.

The service was held on Tuesday, December 16, 2008. It was a cold and rainy day for Los Angeles. Ronn and I both were disappointed that he could not attend due to his work schedule. I had written a speech for the service and was one of four people asked to speak. Mark and Bettie's two nieces were the other speakers. I was also one of the first to arrive and wore a hat because I thought Bettie would like my outfit. Turns out my outfit was a big hit, and I made the *Los Angeles Times* newspaper along with Hugh Hefner.

I didn't know that Bettie's body was in the coffin as she had not been cremated yet. Mark didn't tell me because he thought I would cry. I had crying spells after Bettie finally passed. Even though I expected her death, it still had a tremendous effect on me after all we had gone through in those few weeks at the hospital. So I thought the coffin was just for presentation. It was only later Mark told me he allowed Hefner to see the body and that they made her look really good with a black wig, and that even in death, Bettie had beautiful features.

Mark Roesler started the service with his speech and gave insight to those who didn't know Bettie personally. He talked about taking both Bettie and Anna Nicole Smith to the Playboy Mansion for their fiftieth anniversary party. He said it was always hard to get both of them out of their homes to go anywhere at that time. So a mutual friend named Tommy Sue was helping with Bettie, while he worked on Anna Nicole. He told Anna that Bettie wouldn't go without her, and Tommy Sue told Bettie that Anna wouldn't go without her. So both of them decided to go to the party and that was the only time that Bettie allowed photos to be taken of her in her old age. She never wanted photos of her as an old lady taken; she wanted everyone to remember her from her glorious modeling days. Mark continued his speech saying that Tommy Sue made a comment in the limo to Anna. Tommy Sue said, "Blondes may have more fun, but brunettes get the job done!" Bettie got the biggest kick out of that comment, and we all got a good laugh.

Bettie was essentially the counterpart of Marilyn Monroe, the American pinups from the 1950s, and they will forever be embodied in our minds and in our hearts.

After Mark's speech, it was my turn. Here is what I said:

> Bettie's image meant different things to different people. She was a fantasy to most men and a fashion icon to many women. She was a dear friend to me. I related to her in so many ways, which is why I wanted to meet her and had that honor in the spring of 2002 at Mark Roesler's office.
>
> Bettie and I hit it off immediately due to our southern roots. I wanted to do a documentary on the pinup girl from the pinup girl's point of view. She loved the idea and said I was the first woman to interview her that had also done what she had done in posing nude.
>
> At seventy-eight, I thought she looked much younger, and although her famous bangs were gray, there was no doubt she was the one and only Bettie Page.
>
> Bettie was quite a character. She was very honest and direct in her opinions on nudity, religion, and her disappearance from the

public eye. She was also surprised to learn just how much she had influenced photography, fashion, art, music, and people's perception of sex.

Bettie loved to make us blush, telling us stories of some of the famous men like Howard Hughes who made advances and stories of some of the fetish modeling jobs she did. She had a vivid memory of those days, probably because she enjoyed modeling so much, and used to tell me, "Devin, don't forget to stop and smell the roses."

We occasionally had dinner together, and sometimes I'd cook chili or chicken soup and send over to her, which she loved. I'll never forget going to see the show "The Glory of Christmas" with her and Mark. She just loved those flying angels, and now she is one.

My husband, Ronn Moss, and I were privileged enough to visit her every week in the hospital for the past month before she died. Although she was paralyzed from a stroke and could not speak well at all, she responded to our visits. We would bring her roses from our garden and read the Bible to her, which she loved.

We weren't sure if she understood us and would ask her to blink her eyes if she could. Those bright baby blues would blink, and we would chat with her on what was going on with us. Ronn would wash her face with a cool washcloth because she felt feverish and tell her how loved she is. Bettie seemed to enjoy that personal attention from him.

Then the most amazing thing happened a couple of weeks ago. Ronn and I were on our way to a black-tie wedding and we stopped to visit Bettie. She made quite an effort to talk to us. She told me I looked beautiful, and I said, "Doesn't Ronn look handsome in a tux, Bettie?" She replied, "He looks good in anything!"

We showed her photos of my little dog, Romeo, and she said, "He looks so cute!" We told her about us having horses, and she replied, "I love horses." There was no doubt she understood us and was communicating with us in spite of her failing body. Her mind was still there. We spent about an hour talking to her that day. We told her we were going to a wedding and we would have a dance for her. She of course said, "I love to dance." That visit was an amazing and touching farewell to my friend.

> *I know she will always be in our hearts. I think it's only fitting that Bettie would pass on around Christmastime. Her centerfold of putting the bulb on the Christmas tree is forever etched in our minds, and I will always think of her at Christmastime because of those flying angels. Bettie, if you're flying around with those angels now, don't forget to stop and smell the roses, okay? We love you, Bettie.*

After my speech, Bettie's niece Tammy spoke and told us stories of how fun Bettie was as she was growing up. She said they would play a scary version of hide-and-seek. When Bettie would find them, she would pinch them and make them scream. She talked about how Bettie would make her dolls' clothing with zippers and buttons when she was only ten years old and talked about how talented Bettie was making her own costumes for modeling. She spoke very lovingly of her aunt Bettie, and I thought she inherited her same sparkling baby blues even though she was a natural blonde.

Soon after Bettie's funeral, I decided to inquire about the plot next to hers and found it was available. I decided to buy it so that my final resting place will be right next to my dear friend.

Bettie Page

Bettie Page

Bettie Page

Bettie Page

Author's Bio

Devin DeVasquez was discovered by Playboy and became Miss June 1985. She went on to win $100,000 on the hit talent show *Star Search* and became their 1986 spokesmodel. She also graced *Playboy's* 1986 November cover and celebrity pictorial. She's appeared in film, television, and countless commercials. An actress, producer, director, and writer, Devin is a living example of a successful pinup model.

Printed in the United States
220328BV00002B/3/P